Third Edition

THE
Principal AS
CURRICULUM
LEADER

Third Edition

THE
Principal AS
CURRICULUM
LEADER

Shaping What Is Taught and Tested

ALLAN A. GLATTHORN
JERRY M. JAILALL

CORWIN PRESS
A SAGE Company

For information:

Corwin Press	SAGE India Pvt. Ltd.
A SAGE Company	B 1/I 1 Mohan Cooperative
2455 Teller Road	Industrial Area
Thousand Oaks, California 91320	Mathura Road, New Delhi 110 044
www.corwinpress.com	India
SAGE Ltd.	SAGE Asia-Pacific Pte. Ltd.
1 Oliver's Yard	33 Pekin Street #02-01
55 City Road	Far East Square
London EC1Y 1SP	Singapore 048763
United Kingdom	

Printed in the United States of America.

Library of Congress Cataloging-in-Publication Data

Glatthorn, Allan A., 1924-
    The principal as curriculum leader : shaping what is taught and tested / Allan A. Glatthorn, Jerry Jailall.—3rd ed.
        p. cm.
Includes bibliographical references and index.
ISBN 978-1-4129-6034-2 (cloth)
ISBN 978-1-4129-6035-9 (pbk.)
    1. Curriculum planning—United States. 2. School principals—United States. 3. Educational leadership—United States. 4. School management and organization—United States. I. Jailall, Jerry. II. Title.

LB2806.15.G588 2009
375.001—dc22   2008012029

This book is printed on acid-free paper.

                    11   12   10   9   8   7   6   5   4

Acquisitions Editor:	Arnis Burvikovs
Associate Editor:	Desirée Enayati
Production Editor:	Eric Garner
Copy Editor:	Paula L. Fleming
Typesetter:	C&M Digitals (P) Ltd.
Proofreader:	Carole Quandt
Indexer:	Sheila Bodell
Cover Designer:	Monique Hahn

Contents

Preface to the Third Edition

The third edition provides us with an opportunity to update this book to reflect current developments under the No Child Left Behind (NCLB) legislation and to strengthen sections that, in retrospect, needed greater attention. We have added the most recent research and an expanded list of references related to curriculum and its implementation in the current era of high-stakes accountability. One consequence of NCLB is that it has placed the curriculum at center stage by requiring schools to align curriculum, instruction, and assessment as a basis for securing better student achievement results. Curriculum is at the heart of teaching and learning, and curriculum leadership skills are an essential part of the leadership toolbox to help schools meet Adequate Yearly Progress (AYP) in all student subgroups, including the exceptional children subgroup and English-language learners. Additionally, debates about the inclusion of intelligent design versus evolution in the school curriculum and what 21st-century skills students need in a competitive global economy have raised public consciousness about the content of the school curriculum.

This new edition gives greater attention to the importance of curriculum (or content) standards, since state standards have now been largely institutionalized across the board. We have also addressed the growing chorus for adopting national standards. Chapter 1 has undergone a major revision with updated research and increased focus on the NCLB context relating to curriculum leadership. In Chapter 3, we added a section on the national standards pertaining to school leaders through the influence of national organizations, such as the Interstate School Leaders Licensure Consortium. We also addressed the newly emerging redefined roles and responsibilities of principals in the NCLB and post-NCLB era. In Chapter 5, we added a section on the changing roles of textbooks and digital resources to be considered when selecting instructional materials to support the curriculum. In Chapter 13, a new section addresses some criticisms of constructivism. Throughout, we have referred to the elevation of curriculum reform as an improvement strategy, especially relating to schools and districts under the Title I school improvement sanctions of corrective action and restructuring. Finally, the need for team leadership and professional learning communities in curriculum work is so apparent that this topic receives mention throughout this work.

At a time when principal turnover seems to be high, this book is written specifically for school principals, aspiring principals, and teacher leaders involved in curriculum leadership. This book is derived from several tested beliefs. The first is that there is no single right way to do curriculum. What is offered here, instead, are some useful guidelines tested in practice, not rigid prescriptions. Principals are strongly encouraged to use the guidelines flexibly. The second is that developing and implementing effective curricula are cooperative ventures in which district leaders, school administrators, and classroom teachers should work together toward a common goal. Although this work focuses on the role of the principal, the assumption throughout is that the principal functions as a key player on a cooperative team. The third strong conviction is the need for the principal to play an active leadership role as part of that position's expanding curriculum and instructional leadership responsibilities. Unfortunately, that role has been somewhat ignored in the past literature on educational leadership, but greater attention is now being paid. For students to succeed through mastery of a quality curriculum, the principal must play an active role—at all levels, in all stages. Curriculum leadership is a high-value role that simply cannot be delegated to department heads or content specialists with little input from principals.

The book reflects these basic beliefs. Part I begins with three chapters that provide a foundation by reviewing the knowledge base within the context of state and national standards, examining the four levels of curriculum work, and analyzing the nature and importance of the principal's role. Chapter 1 has been expanded to show how NCLB has ratcheted up the role of the principal as curriculum leader in a standards-based environment.

Part II explains how the principal can influence the state and the district curricula as they are being developed. The changing role of the principal from school manager to learning leader within the NCLB context is addressed.

Part III focuses on the school's curriculum; the argument here is that each school should have its own distinctive curriculum, while still ensuring effective delivery of the district curriculum.

Part IV examines the classroom curriculum and explains how the principal can work with teachers in making the classroom curriculum operational and meaningful.

In Part V, the book closes with a chapter on practical ways of implementing leadership skills.

The purpose of this book is to lay out an overview—a conceptual framework of essential elements to consider when we talk about curriculum. We have sketched the curriculum landscape that aspiring or practicing administrators need to navigate. For detailed, extensive treatment of the curriculum topics in this book, see Allan A. Glatthorn, Floyd Boschee, and Bruce M. Whitehead's *Curriculum leadership: Development and implementation* (Sage Publications, 2006).

Acknowledgments

This third edition acknowledges several individuals who contributed to the previous editions. First, Dr. Glatthorn acknowledges his indebtedness to all the principals with whom he has worked, especially those in the Littleton, Colorado, public schools, who generously shared their experiential wisdom. Second, Dr. Glatthorn's graduate students at East Carolina University, especially the Principal Fellows of 1995–97, have always taught him a great deal about the realities of schools. Dean Casello, of the Raccoon School in Aliquippa, Pennsylvania, was good enough to read the manuscript and give constructive feedback. Gracia Alkema, former president of Corwin Press, provided very useful guidance at the outset of this project.

For this revised third edition, we owe a debt of gratitude to Desirée Enayati, associate editor at Corwin Press, for her patience in guiding the effort and her quest for a quality product. Thanks, too, go to copy editor Paula L. Fleming, who worked diligently to produce the final product; cover designer Monique Hahn; and production editor Eric Garner. We also offer our thanks to Douglas Rife, former president of Corwin Press. Special thanks to all those education leaders who reviewed and made endorsements. Finally, we dedicate this book to our families—our children, our wives, and our brothers and sisters—who have always provided the continuing support we need. Dr. Jailall also makes a special dedication to his mother, Ruby, who has been a continuing source of inspiration.

Special Note

Finally, Corwin Press, SAGE Publications, and coauthor Dr. Jerry Jailall would like to salute the contribution of Dr. Allan Glatthorn, who passed away in September 2007 after a period of illness. He was 83 years old.

To quote from Dr. Jailall's tribute at the funeral:

Dr. Glatthorn was a genius. The education world has lost an intellectual giant, and we have lost a good friend. Dr. Glatthorn may be gone, but his legacy will live on forever. With over 36 books, his contributions to academia are an indelible and universal contribution to the field of leadership, supervision, curriculum, and instruction. Many of his theories and constructs are timeless and will endure in the world of education. His 2006 book on curriculum will be a classic in the field, as well as his book on differentiated supervision. Dr. Glatthorn's style of writing was as clear and concise as it can get, and his books are very user-friendly.

We mourn the loss of Dr. Glatthorn, but at the same time, we celebrate his life and his many years of friendship and fellowship.

Corwin Press would also like to thank the following reviewers:

Harvey Alvy
Singapore American School
Republic of Singapore

Teresa Cunningham, Principal
Laurel Elementary School
Laurel Bloomery, TN

John C. Daresh
University of Texas—El Paso
El Paso, TX

Edward Drugo, Principal
Latrobe Elementary School
Latrobe, PA

Dennis Dunklee
George Mason University
Fairfax, VA

Sheila Fisher, Principal
Maria Weston Chapman
    Middle School
Weymouth, MA

Marian White Hood, Principal
Ernest Just Middle School
Mitchellville, MD

Sylvia Jackson, Principal
Adolfo Camarillo High School
Camarillo, CA

Roger Kaufman
Florida State University
Tallahassee, FL

Fredricka Reisman, Professor
Goodwin College, Drexel
    University
Philadelphia, PA

Pearl Solomon
St. Thomas Aquinas College
Sparkill, NY

Donnan Stoicovy, Principal
Park Forest Elementary School
State College, PA

About the Authors

 Allan A. Glatthorn, EdD, was formerly a distinguished research professor from East Carolina University, Greenville, North Carolina, and a member of the faculty of the University of Pennsylvania Graduate School of Education. For 26 years, he served as a classroom teacher, district supervisor, and high school principal. He is the author of more than 20 professional books on supervision and curriculum, including *Quality Teaching Through Professional Development*, coauthored with Linda Fox and published by Corwin Press. He has consulted with more than 200 school districts, assisting them in developing and implementing their curricula.

 Jerry M. Jailall, EdD, served for 11 years at the North Carolina Department of Public Instruction. He was the state coordinator for the federal Comprehensive School Reform program and a Title I consultant. He has worked with 172 elementary, middle, and high schools implementing school reform initiatives. He previously coordinated the North Carolina School Improvement Grants program in 107 school districts under the standards-based GOALS 2000 federal initiative. He has over 25 years of K–12 experience in public education spanning Guyana, the Bahamas, and the United States. He is a former lecturer at the University of Guyana. He obtained his doctorate in education leadership from East Carolina University.

PART I

Laying the Foundations

CHAPTER ONE

What It Means to Be a Curriculum Leader

No Child Left Behind (NCLB) and Beyond

C urriculum leadership has risen to the forefront with the advent of the bipartisan NCLB Act of 2001. Signed into law in 2002, this federal education legislation has dramatically changed the American educational landscape. It has transformed the nature of school leadership and accountability and redefined school leaders' roles, responsibilities, and authority. One consequence of NCLB is that it has institutionalized the notion that school leaders in the 21st century must be strong curriculum and instructional leaders. Within the context of a global economy, requiring a focus on 21st-century skills and a 21st-century curriculum, NCLB's emphasis on high student achievement for all has been a wakeup call (Mizell, 2005) that has jolted states, districts, and schools to place greater focus on curriculum, instruction, and assessment. In doing so, it has accentuated the role of the principal as a 21st-century curriculum leader. Principals and district leaders are now more publicly accountable for the performance of the students in their schools on high-stakes tests. Schools and districts must show Adequate Yearly Progress (AYP) in student achievement, and results must be publicly reported. A key strategy being used widely to achieve AYP is ensuring that the curriculum is covered and is aligned with the assessments.

In such a high-stakes accountability environment, never before has the curriculum leadership role been so essential to school improvement and reform. Increasing evidence points convincingly to a direct link between the curriculum leadership provided by the principal and leadership team and the effectiveness of the team (Commission on No Child Left Behind, 2007; Sanders & Simpson, 2005; Waters, Marzano, & McNulty, 2003). Attention is being paid to principal preparedness programs and standards for school leadership through the Interstate School Leaders Licensure Consortium (ISLLC) Standards, a national model of leadership standards that serve as common language of leadership expectations across differences in state policies. States have asked the Council of Chief State School Officers (CCSSO) to update the *ISLLC Standards for School Leaders,* published in 1996, to reflect the last decade of policy experience and significant political and social changes. The Council is working with the Interstate Consortium on School Leadership (ICSL) and the National Policy Board for Educational Administration (NPBEA) on a national process to update the standards, with guidance and input being provided by the ICSL members (Sanders & Simpson).

Principals can best discharge their leadership role if they develop a deep and broad knowledge base with respect to curriculum. This chapter first reviews current trends in curricula, especially in relation to state and national standards, and then summarizes the research on curricular quality.

CURRENT TRENDS IN CURRICULA

It is sometimes difficult to distinguish significant trends that are likely to be influential for several years from passing fads that will soon disappear. However, a review of the history of the field and an analysis of the current literature suggest that the following developments are likely to be influential in the first decade of the 21st century.

Increasing Importance of State and National Standards

Discussions of state education standards invariably morph into discussions of national standards for America. The current trend in online learning, including virtual schools, online tutoring, and a plethora of Web-based courses, will trigger discussions about how online learning supplements or is integrated in the school curriculum. This discussion will ultimately loop back to the bigger discussion of state and national standards (see National Education Association, 2002; Nixon, 2007).

NCLB Requires State Standards

In response to the Improving America's Schools Act of 1994 (IASA) and the GOALS 2000: Educate America Act, both of which emphasized standards-based reform, states have set content standards in core subject areas. With the enactment of NCLB, standards-based reform became national education policy (King & Zucker, 2005), and according to Rothman (2004), America embarked on a "de facto national education strategy of reforming schools around standards for student performance" (p. 96).

Under NCLB, as a condition for receiving federal funds, the law requires all states to establish state accountability systems that include challenging academic content, performance standards, and assessments in every grade in grades 3 through 8 and at least once in grades 10 through 12 for reading/language arts and mathematics. Starting in the 2007–2008 school year, students must be assessed in science at least once in grades 3 through 5, once in grades 6 through 9, and once in grades 10 through 12. The standards must specify what children should know and be able to do, contain coherent and rigorous content, and encourage the teaching of advanced skills. NCLB also requires states to align curriculum and assessments and expects continuous progress in achievement by all subgroups of students, who must reach 100 percent proficiency by 2014 (No Child Left Behind Act of 2001). (The reauthorization of NCLB may well see changes in how student performance is measured, given the many recommendations for amendments.)

For instance, California uses Accountability Progress Reporting (APR), an integrated accountability system that reports both the state Academic Performance Index (API) and the federal Adequate Yearly Progress (AYP) and Program Improvement (PI). The API, which tracks the academic performance of schools with a variety of academic measures, is the cornerstone of the accountability system. California Standards Tests (CSTs) are a major component of California's Standardized Testing and Reporting program (STAR).

CSTs measure progress towards state-adopted academic content standards. The California High School Exit Examination (CAHSEE) assesses student performance against the state-adopted content standards for language arts and mathematics; it is a requirement for a California high school diploma.

Under NCLB, failure to make adequate yearly progress (AYP) for two years in a row or more results in schools as well as districts incurring a sequence of escalating sanctions, ranging from being in *school improvement status* to *corrective action* and *restructuring.* Under corrective action, one option is that schools may implement a new curriculum. Under restructuring, schools may replace the principal (NCLB of 2001). Therefore, these sanctions place a spotlight on curriculum and the quality of school leadership.

Until recently, 49 of 50 states had content standards in core subject areas ("Quality Counts," 2003), and now all 50 states have these standards. According to Finn, Petrilli, and Julian (2006), many resources—time, money, and goodwill—have been expended to develop, disseminate, and revise content standards. Several states revise their curricula on scheduled time cycles for different content areas.

Beyond NCLB: Moving From State Standards and Their Unintended Consequences to Voluntary National Standards for States

Unintended Consequences of State Standards

While NCLB has relentlessly kept the focus on student achievement and strong accountability for results, it has spawned some unintended consequences that will need to be addressed during the reauthorization of NCLB and beyond.

Quality and rigor of state content standards varies widely. Spillane (2006) notes that school districts can drown out, minimize, or amplify the impact of standards in schools. Other reviews have found that although a few states have improved their standards, some standards have deteriorated (American Federation of Teachers, 2006; Center on Education Policy, 2007). Finn et al. (2006) find that standards were vague and emphasized skills rather than knowledge. Comparisons of state achievement standards across the nation are difficult to conduct because of wide variations in state tests (Commission on NCLB, 2007).

One commonly expressed concern about NCLB is its effect on subjects not tested and what King and Zucker (2005) call "curriculum narrowing." Studies invariably show that districts and schools have reduced instructional time in at least one subject to increase time on the tested areas of reading and mathematics—the "teaching to the test" syndrome (Center on Education Policy, 2007; National Education Association, 2004; Rentner et al., 2006; Stullich, Eisner, McCrary, & Roney, 2006). Other studies have found increases in time devoted to writing and decreases in time devoted to the arts, foreign languages, and social studies and that high-minority schools seem to be more affected (Mathis, 2003; McGuire, 2007; Vogler, 2003; von Zastrow & Janc, 2004). These and other criticisms abound and form the basis of many recommendations for amendments in the reauthorization of NCLB.

Call for National, Rigorous Standards

However, continuing dissatisfaction with the public schools probably will place pressure on Congress to develop policies that will effect some standardization while still giving primary authority to the states. In a well-balanced analysis, Smith, Fuhrman, and O'Day (1994) summarize the pros and cons of national standards. They cite several advantages claimed by advocates of national standards: such standards will ensure that all citizens will have the shared knowledge and values needed to make democracy work, they result in greater efficiency because they provide standards for the 50 states, they encourage state and local boards to raise their standards, they will improve the quality of schooling, and they will ensure a large measure of educational equity. Similar points are made by Crew, Vallas, and Casserly (2007). It should also be noted that there is some evidence from international comparisons that teachers in nations with strong central control of the curriculum report greater consistency about what should be taught and what they did teach when compared with teachers in nations with greater local control (Cohen & Spillane, 1992). That variation in consistency is probably one of the factors accounting for international differences in achievement.

Smith and colleagues (1994) also note several disadvantages emphasized by the critics of the movement toward a national curriculum: past experience suggests that such attempts will not be effective, standards tend to become minimum standards that lower the entire system, development at the national level will draw resources from state and local efforts, they can lead to an excessively restrictive national curriculum that will inhibit local creativity, and standards alone will have no effect on student achievement unless significant time and resources are provided to local school systems.

Until recently, leveraged by NCLB, almost all states had developed curriculum frameworks and standards (McCabe, 2006), and today, all states have frameworks. And those frameworks seem to be moving from very general guidelines to more prescriptive mandates and are typically accompanied by state-developed tests. A report by Hamilton et al. (2007) that studied California, Georgia, and Pennsylvania concluded that standards-based accountability is leading to "an emphasis on student achievement, and many educators laud this focus" (p. 10). Despite seeming resistance to what is seen as the federalization of education, states, districts, and teacher organizations, such as the American Federation of Teachers (AFT), support state standards and rigor. They nonetheless contend that high-stakes testing alone is not adequate for reform and that other support systems need to be in place (AFT, 2006; Hamilton et al.). This finding is supported by more recent research indicating that teachers seem to accept state standards with a sense of grim resignation (Glatthorn & Fontana, 2000).

Problems in Setting Standards

Several experts have noted problems with states' standard setting in curriculum (see especially Fuhrman, 1994). The standards are set by state officials, who are far removed from local schools and free of the burden of accountability. Curriculum standards are often not supported by other systemic changes, such as new approaches to teacher education. Thus, state initiatives, as random acts of reform, are typically fragmented and often contradictory. And in a time of limited resources and the accompanying downsizing of state staff, most state departments of education do not have the resources to assist local districts in implementing state standards. However, part of the NCLB sanctions for schools and districts that consistently fail to meet AYP targets includes assigning them to escalating levels of school improvement status. This measure is pushing states to design state-level assistance plans for schools and districts in school improvement status, especially for Title I schools.

Although the debate about national standards continues, the patchwork system of state standards and their consequences has led to a louder chorus for national standards. These calls are similar to those made after the report on the 1995 Third International Mathematics and Science Study (TIMSS) showed that many nations outperforming the United States had national standards (Mullis, Martin, Gonzalez, & Chrostowski, 2004). Further motivating this desire is the fact that, overall, states tend to show good gains on state tests but state scores on the National Assessment of Educational Progress (NAEP)—dubbed the "Nation's Report Card"—have been flat or low, despite some modest increases in math (Swanson, 2006). The pendulum swings between a growing consensus on the desirability of state standards and some key resistance to national standards on the grounds of state and local control. A U.S. Chamber of Commerce survey (2006) revealed that 96 percent of business organizations want rigorous curriculum in K–12 classrooms to help prepare students for college and the workplace; less than one-third believe that schools' current state curricula adequately prepare students for their future professional careers (p. 3).

Reports Call for Raising Standards

Crew et al. (2007) argue that states are actually lowering their standards when an avalanche of reports—from the National Academy of Sciences, the U.S. Government Accountability Office, and other entities—suggest that standards need to be raised. They contend that national education standards would give all our schools common targets, clarify what should be taught, give a common definition of academic proficiency, and specify criteria for holding schools and districts accountable. The Council of the Great City Schools (a coalition of 66 of the nation's largest urban school districts), think tanks, and some U.S. legislators proposed a bipartisan plan to provide incentives for states to adopt voluntary education-content standards in math and science. One bill encourages states to benchmark their own standards and tests to the higher standards of the National Assessment of Educational Progress (NAEP) (Crew et al.).

Similarly, the Commission on NCLB report (2007) calls for raising the bar of expectations through the development of national model content and performance standards and tests in reading/language arts, mathematics, and science based on NAEP frameworks. The Commission recommends that for NCLB accountability purposes, states could adopt the resulting national model standards and tests as their own, build their own assessment instruments based on the national model standards, or keep their existing (or revamped) standards and tests.

> States choosing the second or third option would have their standards and tests analyzed and compared to the national model, and the U.S. Secretary of Education will be required to periodically issue reports comparing the rigor of all state standards to the national model using a common metric. (p. 167)

Certainly, the nature of the reauthorized version of NCLB will influence the pace of the dialogue towards creating national education standards. McNeil (2007) reports that the National Conference of State Legislatures voted against any form of national academic standards, including voluntary standards, declaring that any attempt to unite school curricula across states would be unacceptable until perceived flaws in the NCLB Act are fixed.

This is an appropriate place to clarify some terms used by most of the states in their publications and in this book.

- *Curriculum standards or content standards.* Statements of what the learner is expected to be able to do, in one subject, grades K–12. Example (language arts): Uses the reading process to analyze and understand types of literary texts.
- *Benchmarks.* A more specific component of a standard, usually specified for a particular grade or a grade level. Example (language arts, grades 6–8): Understands the features of myths.
- *Objectives.* A component of a benchmark, usually the focus of a given lesson. Example (language arts, grade 6): Identifies the features of a mythical hero.

What should the principal do about state standards? The practical response is to help teachers accept them as a part of their professional work, noting both the advantages and disadvantages of externally imposed standards. State standards should be treated as the floor for curriculum, not the ceiling.

Movement Toward School-Based Curriculum Development

At the same time as interest is increasing in national and state standards setting in curriculum, educators have reported growing interest in school-based curriculum development as one element of the movement toward school-based management and school improvement. Most schools reporting successful school-based management programs indicate that teachers use their decision-making authority to change the program of studies by adding new courses (U.S. General Accounting Office, 1994).

Although one would expect that the concurrent interest in schools of choice would result in greater curricular diversity, one study concludes that there were no major differences between the curricula found in schools of choice and those found in standard schools (Sosniak & Ethington, 1992). Perhaps more diversity in curriculum will be found in the charter school movement, because charter schools are largely free of state curriculum control. A current research project by The National Center on School Choice (2007) with Vanderbilt University and Northwest Evaluation Association (NWEA) is studying the various types of schools of choice with a matched comparison group of regular public schools. The study will compare the curriculum, instruction, and organizational conditions in these schools that promote achievement. It will contrast how schools of choice and regular public schools differ in terms of the content and cognitive complexity of the curriculum and instruction; the differences in alignment among instruction, curricular content standards, and assessments; and how these differences are related to achievement.

NCLB Expands the Core Curriculum

At this point, it is appropriate to mention that beyond the core curriculum of English language arts, mathematics, science, and social studies, NCLB has expanded the core to include foreign languages, civics, government, economics, arts, history, and geography. This expanded list more accurately reflects the demands of 21st-century workplaces, colleges, and communities. It is imperative, therefore, that 21st-century skills be integrated into the teaching and assessment of core subjects.

Greater Influence of Professional Organizations

In previous decades, practitioners did not seem to give much attention to the curriculum recommendations of content area professional groups. Those recommendations often seemed too radical and insensitive to the realities of classroom life. However, the current cry for higher standards seems to have given such recommendations greater credence. Almost all the professional associations representing educators in a particular subject field have published their own curriculum standards. Today, the influence of such organizations is more pronounced. They include the National Council of Teachers of English (NCTE), International Reading Association (IRA), National Reading Conference (NRC), National Council of Teachers of Mathematics (NCTM), National Council for the Social Studies (NCSS), National Science Teachers Association (NSTA), American Council on the Teaching of Foreign Languages (ACTFL), National Art Education Standards (NAES), Mid-continent Research for Education and Learning (McREL), International Society for Technology in Education (ISTE), and others.

A systematic compilation of those professional standards by Kendall and Marzano (2007) indicates that when viewed collectively, they represent an almost impossible task for curriculum leaders. According to Kendall and Marzano's statistics, a student would have to master three benchmarks every week to achieve all the standards set by the professional groups. (A benchmark is a grade-specific and subject-specific standard.) Principals should become familiar with professional standards but encourage their curriculum developers to use them selectively. If the school uses subject-centered teams, the principal should also help team leaders stay current with professional standards.

Continuing Interest in Constructivist Curriculum

Constructivism is a theory of learning based on the principle that learners construct meaning from what they experience; thus, learning is an active, meaning-making process. Though constructivism seems to have made its strongest impact on science and mathematics curricula, leaders in other fields are attempting to embody in curriculum units the following principles:

- The unit should be problem focused, requiring the student to solve open-ended contextualized problems.

- The unit should enable the student to access generative knowledge (knowledge that is used in solving problems).
- Learning strategies (such as the use of matrices in organizing information) should be taught in the context of solving problems.
- Throughout the unit, the teacher should provide the necessary scaffolding or structure.
- Much of the learning should occur in cooperative groups, because learning is a social process.
- The unit should conclude by requiring the student to demonstrate learning in some authentic manner.

Chapter 13 provides a detailed explanation of the processes to be used in developing a constructivist unit and addresses some critiques of constructivism. If greater depth is needed, three sources may be particularly useful: Wiggins & McTighe (2005), Brooks & Brooks (1999), and Glatthorn (1994a).

Development of New Approaches in Vocational Education

In the face of drastic changes in the global economy, the workplace, and the workforce, forward-looking career educators are moving toward new approaches to curriculum to help students develop 21st-century workplace skills. Two developments seem significant.

An Emphasis on Generic Skills

Though almost all career educators see a continuing need to train students in career-specific skills so that they can gain employment after graduation, there is increased interest in so-called generic skills. Generic skills are not job-specific but instead are general, transferable skills that can be used in almost any career. Perhaps one of the best formulations of generic skills is that produced by the Partnership for 21st Century Skills (2007). Its formulation is shown in Table 1.1. As can be seen by reviewing this list (or any other list, such as that by enGauge 21st-Century Skills, 2007), the intent is to equip all students with skills that will enable them to function in a changing 21st-century economy and a changing workplace.

TABLE 1.1

Generic Skills for a 21st-Century Workplace

1. *Mastery of core subjects and 21st-century themes.* These subjects include English, reading or language arts; world languages; arts; mathematics; economics; science; geography; history; and government and civics.

2. *Learning and innovation skills.* These skills prepare students for increasingly complex life and work environments. They include the following:
   - Creativity and innovation
   - Critical thinking and problem solving
   - Communication and collaboration

3. *Information, media, and technology skills.* In a technology- and media-driven environment with an abundance of information, rapid changes in technological tools, and the ability both to collaborate and make individual contributions on an unprecedented scale, students as both citizens and workers must be able to exhibit a range of functional and critical thinking skills, including the following:
   - Information literacy
   - Media literacy
   - Information, communications, and technology (ICT) literacy

4. *Life and career skills.* The ability to navigate the complex life and work environments in the globally competitive information age requires students to pay rigorous attention to developing adequate life and career skills, as well as thinking skills and content knowledge. These skills include the following:
   - Flexibility and adaptability
   - Initiative and self-direction
   - Social and cross-cultural skills
   - Productivity and accountability
   - Leadership and responsibility

SOURCE: Adapted and paraphrased from Partnership for 21st Century Skills (2007).

An Emphasis on Integrating Academic and Career Education

In an attempt to reduce or eliminate the dysfunctional barriers between academic and career curricula, experts in the field are attempting to bring about a greater integration of the two. Eight models of integration have been identified by Grubb, Davis, and Lum (1991); the seven most frequently used models are described briefly here:

1. *Incorporating more academic content in career courses.* Career instructors incorporate into their courses such academic content as reading, writing, science, and mathematics. This has always been done informally by career teachers; there is current interest in developing more systematic models.

2. *Combining career and academic teachers on a teaching team.* In some area career schools, one math teacher and one English teacher will join a team of career teachers, presenting special lessons, working with individual students in a pull-out remedial program, teaching an applied class, and developing materials for the career teachers that reinforce related academic skills.

3. *Making the academic curriculum more career-relevant.* Academic teachers incorporate career applications wherever desirable: reading literature about work, using job-related writing exercises, and using job-related examples from occupational areas, for example. In some cases, this approach is more formalized through the development and implementation of so-called applied academics courses. Three of the most widely used are principles of technology (an applied physics course), applied mathematics, and applied communication. New courses in applied chemistry, applied biology, and materials science and technology are being developed.

4. *Aligning the curricula.* This approach coordinates or aligns closely the content of the career courses and the academic courses; the links between the two fields are strengthened and more clearly delineated. Some curricula use "bridge" assignments, which require the student to complete a project that integrates career and academic knowledge.

5. *Using the senior project as a form of integration.* Some schools are using the senior project as a form of integration. In one school, for example, the student's project consists of a written report; a physical representation of some sort, usually completed in the vocational shop; and an oral presentation, which may include multimedia.

6. *Developing an "academy" model.* Academies usually operate as schools-within-schools. Usually, four teachers collaborate in an academy—one in math, one in English, one in science, and one in the career specialty that is the core of the academy (such as electronics). Other subjects are taken in the regular high school as electives. The teachers work with each other and a single group of students over a multiyear period. The academies establish close ties with local businesses and industries. Grants from the Bill and Melinda Gates Foundation for small schools projects and federal support from the U.S. Department of Education through the Small Learning Communities grants program have promoted the academy model nationally.

7. *Developing occupational high schools and magnet schools.* Magnet schools are similar to academies but the focus on a specialization is schoolwide. Examples are Aviation High School in New York and the High School for Health Professions in Houston.

SOURCE: Grubb, W. N., Davis, G., & Lum, J. (1991). *The cunning hand, the cultured mind: Models for integrating vocational and academic education.* Berkeley, CA: National Center for Research in Vocational Education.

Rather than worrying whether they have the "right" kind of program, principals should evaluate their programs against the following criteria:

- Does the program of studies open doors for all students and not limit opportunities? In too many cases, obsolete vocational programs have not included the academic subjects required for college admissions.
- Do all students have access to reliable career counseling? In many situations, the counseling is not timely, with students being required to make a program choice in grade 9, when such choices are very unstable.
- Do school administrators and teachers make it clear that there are no second-class programs? They should scrupulously avoid making disparaging comments about vocational education, instead according it the same respect as they do academic programs.

Development of Integrated Curricula

Educators seem especially interested in the development and use of curriculum integration as a means of increasing student interest and student knowledge (see Drake & Burns, 2004). Though the concept of curriculum integration is used to mean a variety of approaches, it is used here to denote the development of curriculum units that combine content from two or more disciplines. Though the research generally supports the use of integrated curricula, some problems are associated with their use (see Chapter 9 for a fuller discussion of the research). For that reason, it is recommended that each school decides to what extent and in what ways it will integrate its curriculum. Chapter 9 suggests a process for making that decision.

Institutionalization of Technology

The use of the computer to manage the curriculum and to facilitate student learning is becoming more widely accepted by schools. The issue now is not whether to use technology but which curriculum management program and technologies are most versatile to meet the needs of schools and districts. Except for the few critics of technology, educators generally agree that the use of sophisticated technology will continue to increase in the schools in this rapidly expanding digital age (see Baker, 1999; Davis, Fuller, Jackson, Pittman, & Sweet, 2007; Tomei, 2003).

THE HALLMARKS OF CURRICULUM QUALITY

What constitutes a quality curriculum? In one sense, the question cannot be answered empirically because it deals with values. If principals believe that a narrowly focused curriculum that deals only with the "basics" is most desirable, they will argue for the merits of such a curriculum. On the other hand, if they believe in a comprehensive curriculum that deals broadly with life-related issues, they will advocate that approach. Such a division cannot be reconciled by turning to the research. If that value issue is put aside, however, a number of guidelines for developing a quality curriculum are supported by sound research.

1. *Structure and deliver the curriculum so that it facilitates the mastery of essential skills and knowledge of the subjects.* For many years, educators foolishly argued about the primacy of content or process. Recent advances in cognitive psychology indicate clearly that such a dichotomy is dysfunctional. Students can solve complex problems in science, for example, only when they have a deep knowledge base; but that knowledge base must become generative, not inert, when it is actively processed and used in solving meaningful problems (see Gentile & Lalley, 2003).

2. *Structure the curriculum so that it is closely coordinated.* Several types of coordination seem important: coordination of content, from grades K–12; coordination of the curriculum for one subject, from September to June; coordination within a unit, so that Lesson 3 builds on Lessons 1 and 2 and leads to Lesson 4; and coordination between two related subjects, such as science and mathematics (Erickson, 2007).

3. *Develop an effective integrated curriculum.* As noted above, the extent and nature of such integration should be resolved at the school level. Recent changes in the SAT that introduced a writing component have caused high schools to explore ways to address writing across the curriculum. Similarly, new federal adolescent literacy grants have encouraged across-the-school strategies for developing students' competencies in reading.

4. *Structure the curriculum so that it results in deeper, less superficial coverage.* Several studies conclude that focusing in depth on a smaller number of skills and concepts leads to greater understanding and retention and is also more supportive of efforts to teach problem solving and critical thinking (see Brophy, 1990; Erickson, 2007; Marzano, 2007).

5. *Focus on the mastery of a limited number of essential curriculum objectives rather than trying to cover too many* (Cotton, 1995; Marzano, 2007). Distinguish between those objectives that require specific grade placement, explicit teaching, and systematic assessment and those that should be nurtured on every suitable occasion (Glatthorn, 1994b) (see Chapter 5 for fuller detail).

6. *Organize the curriculum so that it provides for multiyear sequential study, not stand-alone courses.* Though there may be some value in offering stand-alone courses for enrichment purposes at all levels, McDonnell's (1989) research stresses that multiyear, sequential curricula will have greater payoffs than single, fragmented courses.

7. *Emphasize both the academic and the practical.* Johnson (1989) makes this point about the science curriculum: "Generating concepts in the mind . . . should be related where possible to familiar experiences. Experience is the application of understanding" (p. 9). This linking of the academic and the applied should occur throughout the curriculum, not just in "tech prep" courses ("Blending Academic," 2006; Hoachlander, 1999).

8. *Structure the curriculum so that it focuses on problem solving.* Though the initial interest in critical thinking led many innovators to teach isolated thinking skills, the research in cognitive psychology indicates clearly that such skills are better learned and retained when embedded in problem-solving units that deal with complex, meaningful problems situated in a context. (For more detailed discussion of this issue, see Glasgow, 1997; Resnick & Klopfer, 1989; and Torp & Sage, 2002.)

CHAPTER SUMMARY

This chapter lays the foundation by framing the changing role of the principal as that of curriculum leader for 21st-century learning within the context of NCLB and beyond, including the accompanying mandates for high achievement and public accountability and the continuing debate about the viability and usefulness of state and national standards for curriculum. The best response of principals is to deepen their knowledge and process about curriculum, including knowing about current trends in curriculum; being aware of the influence of national curriculum content organizations; knowing how to deepen the integration of technology in the curriculum; knowing how to integrate the academic and vocational curriculum; and ensuring that the school curriculum is grounded by the hallmarks of a quality curriculum, including constructivist learning.

REFERENCES

American Federation of Teachers. (2006, July). *Smart testing: Let's get it right* (Policy Brief No. 19). Washington, DC: Author.

Baker, E. L. (1999). *Technology: Something's coming—something good.* Los Angeles: National Center for Research on Evaluation, Standards, and Student Testing.

Blending academic and real-world learning: An interview with Gary Hoachlander. (2006, summer). *IQ: Irving Quarterly, 6*(1). Retrieved August 19, 2007, from www.irvine.org/publications/iq/archive/vol6 _issue1/youth.shtml

Brooks, J. G., & Brooks, M. G. (1999). *In search of understanding: The case for constructivist classrooms* (Rev. ed.). Alexandria, VA: Association for Supervision and Curriculum Development.

Brophy, J. (1990). Teaching social studies for understanding and higher-order applications. *Elementary School Journal, 90,* 351–417.

Center on Education Policy. (2007, July). *Choices, changes and challenges: Curriculum and instruction in the NCLB era* (A report in the series "From the Capital to the Classroom: Year 5 of the NCLB Act"). Washington, DC: Author.

Cohen, D. K., & Spillane, I. P. (1992). Policy and practice: The relations between governance and instruction. In G. Grant (Ed.), *Review of research in education* (Vol. 18, pp. 3–50). Washington, DC: American Educational Research Association.

Commission on No Child Left Behind. (2007). *Beyond NCLB: Fulfilling the promise to our nation's children.* Washington, DC: The Aspen Institute.

Cotton, K. (1995). *Effective schooling practice: A research synthesis; 1995 update.* Portland, OR: Northwest Regional Educational Laboratory.

Crew, R., Vallas, P., & Casserly, M. (2007, March 5). The case for national standards in American education. *Education Week, 26*(26), 28, 40.

Davis, T., Fuller, M., Jackson, S., Pittman, J., & Sweet, J. (2007). *A national consideration of digital equity.* Washington, DC: International Society for Technology in Education. Retrieved August 13, 2007, from www.iste.org/digitalequity/

Drake, S. M., & Burns, R. C. (2004). *Meeting standards through integrated curriculum.* Alexandria, VA: Association for Supervision and Curriculum Development.

enGauge 21st Century Skills. (n.d.). Retrieved August 19, 2007, from www.metiri.com/features.html

Erickson, H. L. (2007). *Concept-based curriculum and instruction for the thinking classroom.* Thousand Oaks, CA: Corwin Press.

Finn, C. E., Petrilli, M. J., & Julian, L. (2006). *The state of state standards 2006.* Washington, DC: Thomas B. Fordham Foundation.

Fuhrman, S. H. (1994). Legislatures and education policy. In R. F. Elmore & S. H. Fuhrman (Eds.), *The governance of curriculum* (pp. 30–55). Alexandria, VA: Association for Supervision and Curriculum Development.

Gentile, R., & Lalley, J. P. (2003). *Standards and mastery learning: Aligning teaching and assessment so all children can learn.* Thousand Oaks, CA: Corwin Press.

Glasgow, N. A. (1997). *New curriculum for new times: A guide to student-centered, problem-based learning.* Thousand Oaks, CA: Corwin Press.

Glatthorn, A. A. (1994a). Constructivism: Implications for curriculum. *International Journal of Educational Reform, 3,* 449–455.

Glatthorn, A. A. (1994b). *Developing the quality curriculum.* Alexandria, VA: Association for Supervision and Curriculum Development.

Glatthorn, A. A., & Fontana, J. (2000). *Teachers' views of standards and tests.* Washington, DC: National Education Association.

Hamilton, L. S., Stecher, B. M., Marsh, J. A., McCombs, J. S., Robyn, A., Russell, J. L., et al. (2007). *Standards-based accountability under No Child Left Behind: Experiences of teachers and administrators in three states.* Santa Monica, CA: RAND.

Hoachlander, G. (1999, September). *Integrating academic and vocational curriculum—Why is theory so hard to practice?* (CenterPoint Series Number 7). Berkeley: National Center for Research in Vocational Education, University of California—Berkeley.

Johnson, J. R. (1989). *Technology.* Washington, DC: American Association for the Advancement of Science.

Kendall, J. S., & Marzano, R. J. (2007). *Content knowledge: A compendium of standards and benchmarks for K–12 education* (4th ed.). Mid-continent Research for Education and Learning. Retrieved November 6, 2007, from www.mcrel.org/standards-benchmarks/

King, K. V., & Zucker, S. (2005). *Curriculum narrowing* (Harcourt Policy Report). San Antonio, TX: Harcourt Assessment.

Marzano, R. J. (2007). *The art and science of teaching.* Alexandria, VA: Association for Supervision and Curriculum Development.

Mathis, W. J. (2003). No Child Left Behind: Costs and benefits. *Phi Delta Kappan, 84*(9), 679–686.

McCabe, M. (2006, January 5). State of the states: Overview. *Education Week, 25*(17), 72, 74, 76.

McDonnell, L. M. (1989). *Restructuring American schools: The promise and the pitfalls.* New York: Teachers College, Columbia University Institute on Education and the Economy.

McGuire, M. E. (2007, April). What happened to social studies? The disappearing curriculum. *Phi Delta Kappan, 88*(8), 620–624.

McNeil, M. (2007, August 6). NCSL declares opposition to national standards, citing flaws in NCLB. *Education Week, 26*(48). Retrieved August 6, 2007, from www.edweek.org/ew/articles/2007/08/06/45ncsl_web.h26.html

Mizell, H. (2005, December). *An issue of impact: Results of an online survey of educators' experiences with the professional development provisions of the NCLB.* Remarks at National Staff Development Council, Chicago, IL.

Mullis, I. V. S., Martin, M. O., Gonzalez, E. J., & Chrostowski, S. J. (2004). *TIMSS 2003 International mathematics report: Findings from IEA's trends in international mathematics and science study at the fourth and eighth grades.* Chestnut Hill, MA: TIMSS & PIRLS International Study Center, Boston College.

National Center on School Choice. (2007). *National study of schools of choice in NWEA.* Retrieved August 19, 2007, from www.vanderbilt.edu/lsi/proj_nssc_nwea.html

National Education Association. (2002). *Guide to online high school courses.* Retrieved November 6, 2007, from www.nea.org/technology/onlinecourseguide.html

National Education Association. (2004, November). No subject left behind? Think again. *NEA Today, 26*–27.

Nixon, T. (2007). *Complete guide to online high schools: Distance learning options for teens & adults.* Fresno, CA: Degree Press.

No Child Left Behind (NCLB) Act of 2001. 20 U.S.C.A. § 6311 (West 2003).

Partnership for 21st Century Skills. (2007). *Framework for 21st century learnings.* Tucson, AZ. Retrieved March 14, 2008, from www.21stcentury skills.org/documents/frameworkflyer_072307.pdf

Quality counts: "If I can't learn from you" [Special issue]. (2003). *Education Week. 22*(17). Available March 7, 2008, at www.edweek.org/media/ew/qc/archives/QC03full.pdf.

Rentner, D. S., Scott, C., Kober, N., Chudowsky, N., Chudowsky, V., Joftus, S., et al. (2006). *From the capital to the classroom: Year 4 of the No Child Left Behind Act.* Washington, DC: Center on Education Policy.

Resnick, L. B., & Klopfer, L. E. (Eds.). (1989). *Toward the thinking curriculum: Current cognitive research.* Alexandria, VA: Association for Supervision and Curriculum Development.

Rothman, R. (2004). Benchmarking and alignment of state standards and assessments. In S. H. Fuhrman and R. F. Elmore (Eds.), *Redesigning accountability systems for education* (pp. 96–114). Philadelphia, PA: Consortium for Political Research in Education, Teachers College Press.

Sanders, N. M., & Simpson, J. (2005). *State policy framework to develop highly qualified administrators.* Washington, DC: Council of Chief State School Officers.

Smith, M. S., Fuhrman, S. H., & O'Day, J. (1994). National curriculum standards: Are they desirable and feasible? In R. F. Elmore & S. H. Fuhrman (Eds.), *The governance of curriculum* (pp. 12–29). Alexandria, VA: Association for Supervision and Curriculum Development.

Sosniak, L. A., & Ethington, C. A. (1992). When public school "choice" is not academic: Findings from the National Education Longitudinal Study of 1988. *Educational Evaluation and Policy Analysis, 14,* 35–52.

Spillane, J. P. (2006). *Distributed leadership.* San Francisco: Jossey-Bass.

Stullich, S., Eisner, E., McCrary, J., & Roney, C. (2006). *National assessment of Title I: Interim report volume I; Implementation of Title I.* Washington, DC: Institute of Education Studies, U.S. Department of Education.

Swanson, C. B. (2006, January). Making the connection: A decade of standards-based reform and achievement. *Editorial Projects in Education.* Retrieved August 13, 2007, from www.edweek.org/media/ew/qc/2006/MakingtheConnection.pdf

Tomei, L. (2003). *Challenges of teaching with technology across the curriculum: Issues and solutions.* Hershey, PA: Idea Group.

Torp, L., & Sage, S. (2002). *Problems as possibilities: Problem-based learning for K–16 education* (2nd ed.). Alexandria, VA: The Association for Supervision and Curriculum Development.

U.S. Chamber of Commerce. (2006). *Education reform: Insight into the business community's views about the U.S. education system.* Washington, DC: Author.

U.S. General Accounting Office. (1994). *Education reform: School-based management results in changes in instruction and budgeting* (No. 15). Washington, DC: Author.

Vogler, K. (2003). Where does social studies fit in a high-stakes testing environment? *The Social Studies, 94*(5), 207–211.

von Zastrow, C., & Janc, H. (2004). *Academic atrophy: The condition of the liberal arts in America's public schools.* Washington, DC: Council for Basic Education.

Waters, J. T., Marzano, R. J., & McNulty, B. A. (2003). *Balanced leadership: What 30 years of research tells us about the effect of leadership on student achievement.* Aurora, CO: Mid-continent Research for Education and Learning.

Wiggins, G., & McTighe, J. (2005). *Understanding by design* (exp. 2nd ed.). Alexandria, VA: Association for Supervision and Curriculum Development.

CHAPTER TWO

The Four Curriculum Levels

State, District, School, and Classroom

A cold war is being conducted over the control of curriculum. As noted in the previous chapter, especially since the advent of NCLB, state departments of education have become much more active in the area of curriculum, developing detailed standards and high-stakes tests based on standards. At the same time, schools using site-based management are using their authority to develop their own curricula, districts continue to assert their authority over the curriculum, and classroom teachers close the door and teach what they wish to teach. Based on particular state and district contexts, however, districts and schools may feel that they have to cede some local control by getting into lockstep with state-level standards or follow district mandates. As curriculum leader, the principal has to capitalize on any and all opportunities to shape the curriculum in the school.

Rather than siding with one of these claimants for control, this book argues for cooperation among the four levels, based on the belief that each has a part to play. Fuhrman and Elmore (1990) and Togneri and Anderson (2003) point out that curriculum work is performed most effectively when each of the levels exercises its legitimate role in a collaborative manner. If principals understand the function of each level, they can provide effective leadership in their schools. There is evidence that principals understand that curriculum making is a multilevel process. A survey of principals conducted by the National Center for Education Statistics (1995) indicates that public school principals felt that four groups had a "great deal" of influence over curriculum: 61 percent believed that state departments had a great deal of influence; 46 percent, the school board; 49 percent, the principal; and 51 percent, the faculty. Only 7 percent believed that parents had great influence.

In the 2007 Phi Delta Kappa/Gallup Poll on who should have the greatest influence in deciding what is taught in the public schools, the responses were as follows: federal government, 20 percent; state government, 31 percent; and local school board, 49 percent (Rose & Gallup, 2007).

As an overview for what follows in this chapter, Table 2.1 summarizes the functions recommended for each level. Note that Table 2.1 serves also as an organizer for Chapters 6 through 15. Obviously the allocation of these functions should be reviewed closely. Even though the allocations are based on our knowledge of the literature and our experience in consulting with personnel at all four levels, the specific functions undertaken at each level should be determined by state officials, district leaders, principals, and teachers through mutual consultation and dialogue.

STATE FUNCTIONS

Four functions should be performed at the state level:

1. Development of curriculum frameworks

2. Development and implementation of assessment

3. Provision of resources

4. Evaluation

Development of Curriculum Frameworks

The term *curriculum frameworks* is used here in this sense: a set of statements guiding the development and implementation of curriculum and the assessment of student achievement.

Disagreement exists, of course, with respect to the nature and components of state frameworks. Curry and Temple (1992) criticize

TABLE 2.1

Summary of Curriculum Functions by Levels

State Functions

- Develop state frameworks, including broad goals, general standards, and graduation requirements.
- Develop state tests and other performance measures in required academic subjects.
- Provide needed resources to local districts.
- Evaluate state frameworks.

District Functions

- Develop and implement curriculum-related policies.
- Develop a vision of a quality curriculum.
- Develop educational goals based on state goals.
- Identify a common program of studies, the curriculum requirements, and subject time allocations for each level of schooling.
- For each subject, develop the documents for the core or mastery curriculum, including scope and sequence charts and curriculum guides.
- Select instructional materials.
- Develop district curriculum-based tests and other performance measures to supplement state tests.
- Provide fiscal and other resources needed at the school level, including technical assistance.
- Evaluate the curriculum.

School Functions

- Develop the school's vision of a quality curriculum, building on the district's vision.
- Supplement the district's educational goals.
- Develop the school's own program of studies.
- Develop a learning-centered schedule.
- Determine nature and extent of curriculum integration.
- Align the curriculum.
- Monitor and assist in the implementation of the curriculum.

Classroom Functions

- Develop yearly planning calendars.
- Develop units of study.
- Enrich the curriculum and remediate learning.
- Evaluate the curriculum.

"traditional" frameworks for the following reasons: they are too traditional in content and perspective, they are too prescriptive, their elements are not related to each other, they do not address systemic reform, they are too linear and lockstep, and they are presented in a top-down mode. In the place of such traditional frameworks, they propose "progressive" frameworks that emphasize a new view of how students learn and support integration of all components of the curriculum. Curry and Temple argue for comprehensive frameworks, which may include all of the following components: philosophy/rationale/goals, learner and school outcomes, content standards, assessment/student performance standards, themes and concepts of the disciplines, professional development/instructional strategies, instructional technology strategies, sample programs/curriculum units, instructional materials criteria, and interdisciplinary strategies.

We recommend instead more limited frameworks that include only three elements:

1. The broad educational goals that schools are expected to achieve through all programs in 13 years of schooling

2. Graduation requirements in terms of credits and competencies

3. General standards for each required subject

This minimal and general approach is recommended for several reasons. Such an approach gives districts greater autonomy in responding to local needs and strengths, while providing sufficient guidance from the state perspective. It also seems to facilitate district development. Our experience in working with numerous districts in several states suggests that very comprehensive state frameworks are often confusing and counterproductive. Finally, the minimal approach is more efficient in relation to the optimal use of state resources at a time of downsizing in public agencies.

Development and Implementation of Assessment

The second key function of the state is to develop and implement tests and other performance measures. Again a limited approach is recommended, but the reality is that NCLB requires each state to have an assessment system that meets the U.S. Department of Education's stipulations to access federal funds. States should focus their assessment efforts on the following academic subject areas: English language arts, including reading and writing; social studies; science; and mathematics. Also, assessment should be limited to the three transition points: grades 5, 8, and 12. Such a limited approach would give state officials, district leaders, and the public sufficient information to make major decisions without devoting too much time and energy to testing. Studies of the impact of statewide minimum competency assessments conclude that such tests reward harmful instructional practices (such as retention and misuse of special education placement) while not encouraging school improvement (Allington & McGill-Franzen, 1992; Moon, Callahan & Tomlinson, 2003).

In designing and implementing assessment systems, both state and local leaders should make appropriate use of authentic assessments. At the present time, there is widespread interest in moving from paper-and-pencil objective tests to such alternative measures as demonstrations of learning, projects, open-ended problem solving, and portfolios. Some reviews of the research on assessment portfolios conclude that they hold much promise—if developers achieve high levels of technical quality, if educators ensure that the results are not used to perpetuate inequities, and if the developers and users confront honestly the demands that authentic assessment place on evaluators, principals, and teachers.

Provision of Resources

The state should provide school districts with the resources needed to develop and implement quality curricula. Adequate fiscal resources and effective technical assistance seem to be the most important supports the state can provide (Barrett, 2003; Carney, 2001; Herman & Winters, 1994). Depending on established state and district practice, such assistance may include providing state guidelines on the textbook selection and adoption process to support the taught curriculum. The alignment of textbooks with curriculum, instruction, and assessment is an essential part of curriculum leadership.

Evaluation

Finally, state frameworks should be carefully evaluated while they are being produced and after they have been disseminated. Reviewers should consider both professional soundness and feasibility.

DISTRICT FUNCTIONS

Each district needs a consistent program of studies for each level of schooling and a uniform curriculum for each subject. Such consistency and standardization has several advantages. First, it ensures equity across the district: all students receive a quality curriculum, regardless of the school they attend. Second, it facilitates student mobility; students can transfer within the district confident that they will not be penalized because they have missed important content. Third, the district curriculum is more likely to ensure coordination from level to level, and according to Cotton (2003) and the Appalachia Educational Laboratory at Edvantia (2005), such coordination contributes significantly to student achievement. If each school is left to its own devices, breaks in continuity can be expected.

District development of the K–12 curriculum does not preclude school-based curriculum development. In the model advocated here, the district should develop a mastery core curriculum. The mastery core first specifies the subjects that all schools will offer at each grade. Then, for each of those subjects, the mastery core defines the essential skills and knowledge that require explicit teaching and careful structuring. Finally, to enable each school to develop its own curriculum, the district should make supplementary funds available so that every school can add courses to respond to the unique needs of its students.

In identifying the mastery core for each subject, subject matter task forces should develop a sharply focused curriculum that is so integrated and aligned that it does not require more than 80 percent of available time for all students to master. The remaining time is then available for teachers to add their own enrichment.

In achieving a quality curriculum for all students, district leaders should accomplish the tasks identified in Table 2.1 (explained further in Chapter 5). In response to meeting NCLB student achievement targets, the district should not diminish its curriculum leadership role in a quest to secure higher test scores.

SCHOOL FUNCTIONS

Now the school takes over. Schools should resist the temptation merely to adopt the district guide for sake of ease and saving time without enhancing it to meet unique local school needs and priorities. Shaping what is taught in the school requires intentionality. While the state and district set the broader parameters, a school has some scope to customize its curriculum. Under the leadership of the principal and teacher leaders and with appropriate input from parents, the school develops its own curriculum that builds on the district mastery core. The faculty members develop their own vision, identify their own goals, and supplement the district-mandated program by adding courses that respond to the special needs of their students, including exceptional children, migrant children, English-language learners, at-risk students, gifted students, and all student subgroups under NCLB. The principal gets input from the teachers in developing a school schedule that maximizes learning opportunities. The faculty members determine the extent and nature of curriculum integration. They collaborate in aligning the curriculum, developing pacing guides, and monitoring the implementation of the curriculum.

Thus, the school has much important work to do under the leadership of an informed and active principal.

Classroom Functions

Finally, the classroom teachers operationalize the curriculum in several critical ways. They can do this either as individuals or as members of a team or department. They work together in teams or professional learning communities to build yearly planning calendars or pacing guides and then develop units of study and common assessments based on that calendar. They enrich the curriculum, adding to the district curriculum special content that responds to their students' needs and enables them to use their own special knowledge. They remediate learning as the need arises. They implement that enriched curriculum, and they evaluate the curriculum, bringing to bear their own special perspectives.

Flexible Allocations

Although the suggested functions shown in Table 2.1 should work for most school systems, they certainly do not apply to all. It therefore makes sense for principals to cooperate with district leaders in the allocation of functions that better reflect the resources available locally.

With input from teachers, district and school leaders can use this process:

1. Strike out any function that does not seem important for that district.

2. Add any needed functions that have not been listed.

3. Indicate on a form similar to the one shown in Table 2.2 those functions that the state actually performs. (Table 2.2 shows only a portion of the functions that would be listed.)

TABLE 2.2

Example of Allocation of Curriculum Functions

Revised Functions	State	District	School	Classroom
Develop state frameworks	X			
Develop state tests	X			
Develop educational goals	X	X	X	
Identify common program of studies		X		
Develop mastery core curriculum		X		

4. Allocate the remaining functions to the other three levels in a manner responsive to resources and needs. This allocation should result from extensive dialogue and analysis among district staff, school administrators, and teachers.

CHAPTER SUMMARY

This chapter emphasizes that curriculum is a multilevel, shared process involving the state, district, school, and classroom. The cold war over control of the curriculum can be ended by respect for the authority of each level, cooperation across the levels, and systematic planning. Overall, the real action takes place at the school and classroom levels where the principal has a key role to play, as shown in the next chapter.

REFERENCES

Allington, R. L., & McGill-Franzen, A. (1992). Does high-stakes testing improve school effectiveness? *ERS Spectrum, 10*(2), 3–12.

Appalachia Educational Laboratory at Edvantia. (2005). *Research brief: Components of school capacity; Structures, practices, and perceptions.* Retrieved September 10, 2007, from www.edvantia.org/pdta/pdf/School_Capacity.pdf

Barrett, H. C. (2003). *The research on portfolios in education.* Retrieved September 10, 2007, from http://electronicportfolios.com/ALI/research.html

Carney, J. (2001). *Electronic and traditional portfolios as tools for teacher knowledge representation.* Unpublished doctoral dissertation, University of Washington, Seattle.

Cotton, K. (2003). *Principals and student achievement: What the research says.* Alexandria, VA: Association for Supervision and Curriculum Development.

Curry, B., & Temple, T. (1992). *Using curriculum frameworks for systemic reform.* Alexandria, VA: Association for Supervision and Curriculum Development.

Fuhrman, S. H., & Elmore, F. (1990). Understanding local control in the wake of state education reform. *Educational Evaluation and Policy Analysis, 12,* 82–96.

Herman, I. L., & Winters, L. (1994). Portfolio research: A slim collection. *Educational Leadership, 52*(2), 48–55.

Moon, T. R., Callahan, C. M., & Tomlinson, C. A. (2003, April 28). Effects of state testing programs on elementary schools with high concentrations of student poverty: Good news or bad news? *Current Issues in Education, 6*(8). Retrieved October 1, 2007, from http://cie.ed.asu.edu/volume6/number8/

National Center for Education Statistics. (1995). *Who influences decision making about curriculum: What do principals say?* Washington, DC: Author.

Rose, L. C., & Gallup, A. M. (2007). *The 39th annual Phi Delta Kappa/Gallup poll of the public's attitudes toward the public schools.*

Retrieved September 22, 2007, from www.pdkintl.org/gallup/PDK_ Gallup_Poll_39_EMB.pdf

Togneri, W., & Anderson, S. E. (2003). *Beyond islands of excellence: What districts can do to improve instruction and achievement in all schools—a leadership brief* (A project of the Learning First alliance). Alexandria, VA: Association of Supervision and Curriculum Development.

CHAPTER THREE

Importance of the Principal

T o serve as effective leaders of curriculum, school administrators need to have more than a passing knowledge of curriculum and understand the importance of their role in this area. This chapter begins by outlining national standards for leadership and changing roles, defines briefly the concept of curriculum leadership, and notes the problems that face principals in executing this role. The chapter continues by presenting a rationale for the importance of curriculum leadership and indicates how principal leadership can be joined with teacher leadership in effective collaboration. The chapter concludes by suggesting some specific ways by which the principal can discharge the leadership function.

NCLB COMMISSION REPORT CALLS FOR DEFINITION OF *HIGHLY EFFECTIVE PRINCIPALS*

After the advent of NCLB, in the quest for higher student achievement, increased attention has been paid to the role of the principal as a curriculum leader. The Commission on No Child Left Behind recommends establishing, as a new aspect of NCLB, a definition for Highly Effective Principals (HEP). The Commission links teacher quality to principal quality and envisages an effective principal as someone who can drive change, can accelerate and sustain high student achievement, and is skilled enough to turn around low-performing schools (Commission on NCLB, 2007).

Educators are focused on the effectiveness of the current leadership preparation design and process, including what has been known over the years as the ISLLC (Interstate School Leaders Licensure Consortium) standards. The expectation is that the licensure process should ensure that principals have the skills to promote 21st-century learning, leading to higher student achievement and the attainment of Adequate Yearly Progress (AYP).

REVISED NATIONAL EDUCATIONAL LEADERSHIP POLICY STANDARDS: ISLLC 2008

The Interstate School Leaders Licensure Consortium (ISLLC) *Standards for School Leaders* (Council of Chief State School Officers, 1996) was written by representatives from states and professional associations in partnership with the National Board for Educational Administration in 1994–95 and published by the Council of Chief State School Officers (CCSSO) in 1996.

A 2006 CCSSO survey shows that 49 states have leadership standards for administrator certification and leadership practice and preparation programs. Of these, 43 states report that they adopted or adapted the ISLLC *Standards* or confirmed alignment of their state standards with ISLLC (CCSSO, 2007).

The ISLLC *Standards* have become a national model embodying the vision of the new education leader. They provide a common language of leadership expectations across states and recast the roles of leaders to include school improvement and attention to teaching and learning. According to Murphy (2002), the consortium's standards provide the "DNA" for reculturing the profession of school administration by providing a platform for the reconstitution of leadership preparation programs and for certification and recertification of school leaders.

Thus, the era of NCLB has spurred the redirection of leaders from the *management* of schools to the *leadership* of schools (Murphy, 2002), including a focus on curriculum and instruction.

In December 2007, CCSSO released a revised document, *Educational Leadership Policy Standards: ISLLC 2008,* which was adopted by the National Policy Board of Educational Administration (NPBEA). These standards, clustered around six major areas, are intended to give policymakers and education leaders a common vision and goals for how to improve student achievement through better educational leadership. They further are intended to guide the licensure and assessment process and drive the practice standards of school executives (CCSSO, 2008).

According to Portin, Alejano, Knapp, and Marzolf (2006), states have statutory language and guidance linked to the ISLLC *Standards,* so updating them has significant implications for state certification policies, leadership programs, professional assessments, and policy system alignment.

In 2008, the NPBEA members were the following major organizations involved in policymaking for school leadership: the American Association of Colleges for Teacher Education (AACTE), Association for Supervision and Curriculum Development (ASCD), National Council on Accreditation of Teacher Education (NCATE), National Association of Elementary School Principals (NAESP), American Association of School Administrators (AASA), National Association of Secondary School Principals (NASSP), National Council of Professors of Educational Administration (NCPEA), National School Boards Association (NSBA), University Council for Educational Administration (UCEA), and the Council of Chief State School Officers (CCSSO) (CCSSO, 2008).

Retooling for Curriculum Leadership Under NCLB and Beyond

Schools and districts have retooled curriculum and instructional programs to improve teaching and learning. Thus, we find educators mapping the curriculum to align with state standards (including using curriculum-mapping software programs) and adopting new curriculum materials, and special education and regular education teachers are collaborating more (Goertz & Massell, 2005; Rentner et al., 2006). Curriculum, instruction, and assessments are more interconnected through the use of standards. Educators are more focused on providing all students with access to a comprehensive and challenging curriculum—one of the elements identified in research as a key to closing achievement gaps (Seidel & Short, 2005).

Leadership that is focused on and accountable for learning is the genesis of such phrases as *leading for learning, learning-focused leadership,* and *learner centered* accountability (see Darling-Hammond, 1997; DuFour, 2002; Knapp, Copland, Darling-Hammond, McLaughlin, & Talbert, 2002). School leaders find themselves engaged in the reculturation of the schools and, concomitantly, involved in the redesign of school schedules, staffing configurations, student assignment, and curriculum, among other factors forming the educational environment.

In the arena of high school improvement, the American Association of School Administrators (AASA) advocates that improvement efforts should focus on curriculum that is thorough and robust and provides a connection to the real world for students, as well as focusing on the relationships among students and between students and adults in the school (AASA, 2007, #38). Others advocate a restructured curriculum with Advanced Placement courses, or International Baccalaureate programs, as a means of achieving educational equity between poor and affluent students, enabling more students to be college-ready (see Matthews & Hill, 2005). Also, at the high school level, principals need to be able to assess the curriculum content of the wide range of online courses and other online learning that is increasingly available to students.

Redefining Roles, Responsibilities, and Authority of School Leaders

According to Leithwood & Riehl (2003), the idea that the principal provides a nexus of innovative ideas, resource acquisition, and empowerment continues to hold a prominent place in policy and practice. In this debate, some argue that managerial expertise trumps instructional know-how, especially in leading turnaround schools, while others assert the importance of having a deep understanding of teaching and learning. Sanders & Simpson (2006) contend that curriculum leadership demands a broad set of transformational skills that, used interchangeably, support, challenge, and influence staff. Marzano, Walters, & McNulty (2005) found that principal leadership is significantly correlated with student achievement. As noted earlier, the Commission on NCLB, in focusing on principal quality, wants to go beyond the"highly qualified" designation based on the licensure process and recommends establishing a definition for Highly Effective Principal (HEP) (Commission on NCLB, 2007).

DEFINING CURRICULUM LEADERSHIP

The term *curriculum leadership* is used in this book in the following sense: the exercise of those functions that enable school systems and the schools to achieve their goal of ensuring quality in what students learn. Several aspects of this definition require attention.

First, the definition emphasizes functions, not roles. Whereas the role of the principal has been the emphasis of this text, superintendents, assistant superintendents, central office supervisors, principals, assistant principals, department chairs, team leaders, and classroom teachers all have a part to play as well.

Second, it emphasizes leadership of those processes that enable systems and individuals to achieve their goals. The functions are goal oriented instead of being a set of routine, mindlessly taken steps. And the ultimate goal is maximizing student learning by providing quality content. Thus, this work makes a clear distinction between curriculum (what is learned) and instruction (how the content is taught).

UNDERSTANDING THE PROBLEMS OF THE PRINCIPAL'S CURRICULUM LEADERSHIP ROLE

Several problems confront school administrators interested in discharging this role. The first is lack of clarity about its nature. Principals seem to encounter problems when trying to understand definitely what being a curriculum leader means. In workshops we have conducted, principals have expressed uncertainty about the specific nature of curriculum leadership, often suggesting that curriculum is a district concern, not a school issue.

This attitude of "curriculum is not my job" has perhaps been intensified by the promulgation of state standards. Although state standards and state tests limit the authority of both the district and the school, many key functions nonetheless need to be discharged by the principal and the teachers. Any belief by principals that they have no influence on the district curriculum becomes a self-fulfilling prophecy.

The second difficulty is lack of time. Even when principals are generally aware of their curriculum responsibilities, they have difficulty finding the time to execute the role. In one study, high school principals reported that "program development" was first on their list of what they should spend time on but fourth in terms of time actually spent (Pellicer, Anderson, Keefe, Kelley, & McCleary, 1988). Principals report spending the largest proportion of their time

(35 percent) on guiding and motivating teachers, 24 percent on reporting and compliance, and 20 percent on discipline, with all three areas accounting for 77 percent of their time (MetLife Survey of the American Teacher, 2006).

Finally, principals do not seem to be receiving much help from the experts in understanding curriculum leadership. The literature on the role of the principal as a curriculum leader is surprisingly limited. Though there seem to be hundreds of articles and books dealing with instructional leadership, a recent search of the Education Resources Information Center (ERIC) database on the leadership role of the principal in curriculum revealed only a small number of sources. It would seem that most experts who have examined school leadership have focused unduly on the principal as a leader of instruction, ignoring the role of curriculum leader. A notable exception here is English's (1992) book.

This book attempts to address this vacancy in the literature. It analyzes systematically the nature of the principal's curriculum leadership role, indicates clearly what steps need to be taken in discharging it, and suggests how principals can find time to serve as curriculum leaders.

UNDERSTANDING THE RATIONALE FOR PRINCIPAL LEADERSHIP

Why should the principal serve as a curriculum leader? The answer is based on several tested assumptions. First, a quality curriculum is essential in achieving educational excellence. Though this assumption has the appeal of common sense, it is also supported by sound research. By reviewing more than 3,000 studies of student achievement, Fraser, Walberg, Welch, and Hattie (1987) identified the quality of the curriculum as one of ten factors influencing student achievement (see also Cotton, 1995, for a summary of the research here). The best teaching methods, when used to deliver poor content, result only in a great deal of mislearning.

Second, though both the state and the district have key roles to play in the development and implementation of curriculum, there is widespread agreement among the experts that meaningful change takes place primarily at the school level (see Fullan, 2006; Glickman,

1993; Newmann & Wehlage, 1995; Schlechty, 2005). As explained in the previous chapter, the best curriculum work integrates functions at several levels—state, district, school, and classroom.

Also, abundant evidence suggests that the principal plays a key role in determining the overall effectiveness of the school. As will be noted later, teachers can work with the principal collaboratively in discharging vital leadership functions. However, even in the best teacher leadership models, there is a strong need for the principal to provide ongoing leadership, as noted by Murphy (2005).

Hord and Hall (1983) and Hall and Hord (2006) conclude that strong leadership on the part of the principal plays a key role in determining the extent of curriculum leadership. They also discovered that principals who used an active initiating style are most effective in ensuring effective implementation. Principals with this style

- have clear long-range policies and goals;
- have strong expectations for students, as well as convey and monitor those expectations;
- seek changes in district programs and policies; and
- solicit input from staff but act decisively

UNITING PRINCIPAL AND TEACHER LEADERSHIP

A great deal of interest currently exists in implementing models of teacher leadership (see Glickman, 2002; Stave & Black, 2001).

Unfortunately, most of the models of teacher leadership seem to suggest that it occurs in a vacuum, removed from the world of the principal. Wasley's work (1991) and Murphy's (2005) are exceptions, however.

Wasley's case studies of teacher leaders conclude that administrative support and collaboration are essential if such programs are to be effective. In support of Wasley's findings, our experience in working with school districts to improve curriculum indicates clearly that leadership should be exercised collaboratively and flexibly. Collaboration is essential, because the tasks are manifold and multiple perspectives are vital. Flexibility is crucial, because contextual elements vary so much. To ensure both collaboration and flexibility, the principal and the teachers together should analyze the following factors in determining the balance between principal and teacher leadership:

- The personnel resources available from the central office
- The extent of curriculum work at the district level
- The total responsibilities of the principal
- The other administrative help available to the principal
- The curriculum priorities at the school level
- The extent to which teachers are interested in curriculum leadership
- The existence of professional learning communities in the school
- The time and other resources available to teachers

One way of operationalizing this analysis is to use the form shown in Table 3.1. The form lists all the functions specified for both the school and the classroom curriculum. (The list presented here should be checked against the master list developed using Table 2.1 to be sure that they are congruent.) The principal should initiate the process by discussing it in a general faculty meeting. At that time, the principal can emphasize the importance of collaboration, explain the nature of each function, and clarify how teachers can provide input. (Chapters 6 through 15 provide detailed information with respect to each of these functions.) After this orientation session, the principal should complete the form as indicated and then distribute it to the faculty to gather their responses. When all responses have been tallied and summarized, the principal should confer with team leaders (a generic term that includes department or grade-level chairs) to analyze the results and build the local school model of curricular leadership.

Discharging the Leadership Functions

Once the leadership functions have been delineated, the principal can best discharge those functions by keeping in mind two general recommendations. The first is to use the routine acts that consume the typical day as occasions for curriculum emphasis. Scott, Ahadi, and Krug (1990) determined that principals who were most effective in discharging instructional leadership (which the authors defined as including curriculum leadership) did not use different behaviors than

TABLE 3.1

Analyzing Curriculum Leadership Roles

Directions: Listed below are the essential functions of curriculum leadership as they should be carried out at the school and classroom levels. For each function, determine what role each of the individuals or groups noted on the chart should play. Use this code in responding:

L: This individual or group should lead in discharging this function.

C: This individual or group should contribute to this function.

Leave the space blank if you believe that this individual or group should play no role at all.

Function	DS	P	AP	TL	T
School Functions					
1. Develop the school's vision of a quality curriculum, building on the district's vision.					
2. Supplement the district's educational goals.					
3. Develop the school's own program of studies.					
4. Develop a learning-centered schedule.					
5. Determine the nature and extent of curriculum integration.					
6. Align the curriculum.					
7. Monitor and assist in the implementation of the curriculum.					

Code: DS = district supervisor; P = principal; AP = assistant principal; TL = team leaders and department chairs; T = classroom teachers

(Continued)

(Continued)

Function	DS	P	AP	TL	T
Classroom Functions					
1. Develop yearly planning calendars for operationalizing the curriculum.					
2. Develop units of study.					
3. Enrich the curriculum and remediate learning.					
4. Evaluate the curriculum.					

less effective principals used; instead, they used routine behaviors as opportunities for curriculum emphasis and gave their routine actions a curricular interpretation. For example, in monitoring the student cafeteria, they would talk with students about what they were learning and how they felt about their subjects.

The second recommendation is that the principal understand that curriculum leadership does not exist in a vacuum but is simply one component of effective organizational behavior. In their studies of effective curriculum leaders, Aronstein and DeBenedictis (1988) and Marzano et al. (2005) determined that such principals use behaviors that have a schoolwide impact rather than a narrowly focused curriculum emphasis. Aronstein and DeBenedictis identify five "enabling behaviors" that make a schoolwide difference:

1. Facilitating communication

2. Creating a positive, open climate

3. Building a vision with the staff

4. Developing staff through involvement

5. Being an effective and positive role model

Additional suggestions for operationalizing the principal's role can be found in Chapter 16.

CHAPTER SUMMARY

The advent of NCLB and the push for higher student achievement has put more focus on national standards for school leadership, and the adequacy of current principal preparation programs in producing not just highly qualified but highly effective school leaders is being evaluated. The role of principals is tilting more towards providing curriculum and instructional leadership for school improvement in addition to the usual managerial functions. School leaders, in partnership with teacher leaders and other professional learning communities within the school, can be highly effective in discharging the leadership functions for curriculum and instruction. Such empowering relationships may help shape state and district curriculum practices, as will be discussed in Part II.

REFERENCES

The American Association of School Administrators (AASA). (2007). *AASA position statements.* Retrieved October 7, 2007, from www.aasa.org/files/PDFs/GovDocs/AASAPositionStatements072007.pdf

Aronstein, L. W., & DeBenedictis, K. L. (1988). *The principal as a leader of curriculum change: A study of exemplary school administrators.* Quincy: Massachusetts State Department of Education.

Commission on No Child Left Behind (NCLB). (2007). *Beyond NCLB: Fulfilling the promise to our nation's children.* Washington, DC: The Aspen Institute.

Cotton, K. (1995). *Effective schooling practices: A research synthesis; 1995 update.* Portland, OR: Northwest Regional Educational Laboratory.

Council of Chief State School Officers (CCSSO). (1996). *Interstate School Leaders Licensure Consortium (ISLLC) Standards for School Leaders.* Washington, DC: Author. Available March 23, 2008, at www.ccsso.org/content/pdfs/isllcstd.pdf

Council of Chief State School Officers (CCSSO). (2007). *Key state education policies on PK–12 education: 2006.* Washington, DC: Author. Retrieved October 6, 2007, from www.ccsso.org/publications/details.cfm?PublicationID=348

Council of Chief State School Officers (CCSSO). (2008, March). *Introduction to the educational leadership policy standards: ISLLC 2008.* Washington, DC: Author. Retrieved March 19, 2008, from www.ccsso.org/projects/education_leadership_initiatives/

Darling-Hammond, L. (1997). *The right to learn: A blueprint for creating schools that work.* San Francisco: Jossey-Bass.

DuFour, Richard. (2002). The learning-centered principal. *Educational Leadership, 59*(8), 12–15.

English, F. W. (1992). *Deciding what to teach and test: Developing, aligning, and auditing the curriculum.* Thousand Oaks, CA: Corwin Press.

Fraser, B. J., Walberg, H. J., Welch, W. W., & Hattie, J. A. (1987). Syntheses of educational productivity research. *International Journal of Education, 11,* 145–152.

Fullan, M. (2006). *Breakthrough.* Thousand Oaks, CA: Corwin Press.

Glickman, C. D. (1993). *Renewing America's schools.* San Francisco: Jossey-Bass.

Glickman, C. D. (2002). *Leadership for learning: How to help teachers succeed.* Alexandria, VA: Association of Supervision and Curriculum Development.

Goertz, M., & Massell, D. (2005). Summary. In B. Gross & M. Goertz (Eds.), *Holding high hopes: How high schools respond to state accountability policies* (CPRE Research Report Series RR-056, pp. 123–134). Philadelphia: Consortium for Policy Research in Education. Retrieved September 15, 2007, from www.cpre.org/images/stories/cpre_pdfs/rr56.pdf

Hall, G. E., & Hord, S. M. (2006). *Implementing change: Patterns, principles, and potholes* (2nd ed.). Boston: Allyn & Bacon.

Hord, S. M., & Hall, G. E. (1983). *Three images: What principals do in curriculum implementation.* Austin: University of Texas, Research and Development Center for Teacher Education.

Knapp, M. S., Copland, M. A., Darling-Hammond, L., McLaughlin, M. W., & Talbert, J. E. (2002, April). *Leadership for teaching and learning: A framework for research and action.* Paper presented at the annual meeting of the American Educational Research Association, New Orleans, LA.

Leithwood, K. A., & Riehl, C. (2003, April). *What do we already know about successful school leadership?* Paper presented at the annual meeting of the American Educational Research Association, Chicago. Retrieved September 15, 2007, from www.cepa.gse.rutgers.edu/What We Know _long_ 2003.pdf

Marzano, R. J., Walters, T., & McNulty, B. (2005). *School leadership that works: From research to results.* Alexandria, VA: Association for Supervision and Curriculum Development.

Matthews, J., & Hill, I. (2005). *Supertest: How the International Baccalaureate can strengthen our schools.* Peru, IL: Carus.

Metropolitan Life Insurance Company. (2006). *The MetLife survey of the American teacher: Expectations and experiences; A survey of teachers, principals and leaders of college education programs.* New York: Author. (ERIC Document Reproduction Service No. ED496558)

Murphy, J. (2002). Reculturing the profession of educational leadership: New blueprints. *Educational Administration Quarterly, 38*(2), 176–191.

Murphy, J. (2003, September). *Reculturing educational leadership: The ISLLC* Standards *ten years out.* Paper prepared for the National Board for Educational Administration. Available March 8, 2008, at www .npbea.org/Resources/ISLLC_10_years_9–03.pdf

Murphy, J. (2005). *Connecting teacher leadership and school improvement.* Thousand Oaks, CA: Corwin Press.

Newmann, F. M., & Wehlage, G. G. (1995). *Successful school restructuring.* Madison: University of Wisconsin, Center on Organization and Restructuring of Schools.

Pellicer, L. O., Anderson, L. W., Keefe, J. W., Kelley, E. A., & McCleary, L. E. (1988). *High school leaders and their schools: Vol 1. A national profile.* Reston, VA: National Association of Secondary School Principals.

Portin, B. S., Alejano, C. R., Knapp, M. S., & Marzolf, E. (2006, October). *Redefining roles, responsibilities, and authority of school leaders.* Seattle: University of Washington, Center for the Study of Teaching and Policy. Available March 8, 2008, at http://depts.washingon.edu/ctpmail/PDFs/Roles-Oct16.pdf

Rentner, D. S., Scott, C., Kober, N., Chudowsky, N., Chudowsky, V., Joftus, S., et al. (2006). *From the capital to the classroom: Year 4 of the No Child Left Behind Act.* Washington, DC: Center on Education Policy.

Sanders, N. M., & Simpson, J. (2006). *Information and handouts for state education agencies: Updating the ISLLC standards for school leaders and the ELCC/NCATE program standards.* Washington, DC: Council of Chief State School Officers. Retrieved October 7, 2007, from www.ccsso.org/content/PDFs/Talking Points3.20.06.pdf

Schlechty, P. C. (2005). *Creating great schools: Six critical systems at the heart of educational innovation.* San Francisco: Jossey Bass.

Scott, C., Ahadi, S., & Krug, S. E. (1990). *The experience sampling approach to the study of principal instructional behavior: Vol. 2.* Urbana, IL: National Center for School Leadership.

Seidel, K., & Short, E. (2005). *Connecting students, standards, and success: Using standards-based curriculum connections to improve learning.* Retrieved September 15, 2007, from www.acr.uc.edu/acr _pdf/StudentsStandards_Success[2].pdf

Stave, A., & Black, A. (2001). Action research: A model for teacher leadership through the NCATE review process. *Educational Horizons, 79*(3), 130–134.

Wasley, P. A. (1991). *Teachers who lead.* New York: Teachers College Press.

PART II

Shaping State and District Curricula

Chapter Four

State Policies and Frameworks

As explained in Chapter 2, the state has a legitimate role to play in the development of curriculum policies and frameworks. It is here that principals need to be proactive, influencing those foundation documents as they are being developed rather than only responding reactively after they have been finalized. Principals also have a role in evaluating state documents once they have been published. The point of view advanced here is that principals have a professional responsibility to exercise their influence at the state level.

BECOMING INFORMED

The first step is to become informed about state initiatives as they are being developed. Three kinds of information are crucial. First, principals need to keep informed in advance about new initiatives under development. The state professional association is the best source for this information.

Second, they need to understand the political and legislative processes in their states. That knowledge embraces both the formal processes that are explicated in the law and, even more importantly, includes the informal processes that really get things done. State policy making operates through informal contacts, through discussions with lobbyists and pressure groups, and through behind-the-scenes negotiating and bargaining.

Finally, they need to stay informed about the best research on current educational reforms. Principals can speak and write more persuasively if they do so from an informed perspective. The best sources here are the professional journals. Other useful sources include *Education Week* and the online blogs and discussion groups of national organizations.

GETTING THE MESSAGE ACROSS

With that knowledge, principals can then work at communicating their views to state legislators, state board of education members, and other policy makers. They can do this both as members of professional associations, most of which have their own lobbyists, and as individuals. Some states have published schedules for curriculum revisions, and principals need to be strategic in making sure their voices are heard timely. Some states also have advisory committees for curriculum that provide a forum for input.

Principals cannot simply say that they are too busy to be involved in shaping policy about curriculum. Advocacy is an essential function of the effective school leader.

In working with professional groups, principals should encourage them to develop and disseminate policy briefings. These are documents written for state and local policy makers on the vital educational issues being examined for possible action (see Glatthorn, 1996, as an example of this type of document, written for North Carolina policy makers on the issue of charter schools). The policy briefings will be most effective if they are objective and unbiased, if they cite the evidence, if they are brief and to the point, and if they are in the hands of legislators immediately prior to their consideration of proposed legislation.

In speaking and writing individually to policy makers, principals should keep in mind certain commonsense guidelines about such communication:

- Say it in your own words. Legislators quickly recognize canned messages.
- Keep the message brief and to the point. Policy makers are busy people; they usually will not read lengthy documents.
- Use a professional tone. Use language that is courteous, respectful, and objective.

- Communicate persuasively. Analyze the values. Examine the issues. Provide the evidence.
- Be sure the form is perfect. Have someone check the letter or e-mail message for spelling, punctuation, and sentence structure.

A letter that exemplifies these qualities is shown in Figure 4.1.

Figure 4.1   Letter to Legislator

Dear Senator Bridges:

I write to you as a constituent and as a concerned educator about Senate Bill 1045, "Authorization for Later Opening Date for Schools," to be proposed for action during the May special session.

Although the concept of "saving our summers" is potentially an attractive one, I believe that additional study of its impact on planning time is needed before the state authorizes this bill. It is important that our planning time is protected.

SB 1045 requires the following changes in how local school boards determine the traditional school calendar:

1. Requires schools to open for students no earlier than August 25 and end no later than June 10.

2. Reduces the number of required days in the school calendar from 220 to 215 by eliminating 5 teacher workdays from the school calendar.

3. Requires that five workdays be restricted to instructional and classroom administrative duties. Local units would not be allowed to impose any additional tasks on those days. One of these days would have to be at the beginning of the school year and one at the end of the school year.

The loss of the five teacher workdays would seriously affect our work in curriculum development and planning as well as other related, necessary professional development activities. I would be happy to provide you with additional information about these issues if you and your colleagues desire it.

I would much appreciate it if you would see fit to vote NO on changing the opening date for schools, if this means losing five teacher workdays.

Thanks for your kind consideration.

Sincerely,

Principal

Phone:

E-mail:

EVALUATING STATE FRAMEWORKS

In addition to influencing state policy making in a proactive fashion, principals should also participate in the evaluation of state materials once they have been developed by department of education staffs. In assessing state frameworks, the following criteria can be used:

- Do the frameworks represent the best current professional thinking and reflect sound empirical research? (Too many frameworks seem excessively responsive to passing fads.)
- Do the frameworks provide a reasonable measure of state direction while still giving local districts sufficient autonomy? (Several state frameworks seem highly controlling and overly specific.)
- Are the state frameworks easy to use at the local level? (Several state frameworks seem excessively complicated, making the work of the local district exceedingly difficult.)
- Are the elements of the state frameworks compatible and coherent? (One state curriculum guide for reading emphasized that each reader should bring to bear his or her unique experience in interpreting a literary passage; however, the state test asked students to choose the "correct" interpretation of a passage from among four alternatives.)
- What is the evidence that the state frameworks will have a significant impact on student learning? (Some state frameworks deal with peripheral elements that will probably not have an impact on student learning.)

CHAPTER SUMMARY

This chapter focused on the principal having some responsibility as an advocate, individually or through professional organizations, to influence state curricula. Principals must be knowledgeable about state curriculum frameworks and their revision cycles, be familiar with the research on curriculum, and be able to evaluate curricular effectiveness with a view of contributing informed input to the decision-making process. Armed with knowledge of the state-level curriculum process, principals are better able to influence the district-level curriculum process, as discussed in the next chapter.

REFERENCE

Glatthorn, A. A. (1996). *Policy brief: Charter schools.* Greenville, NC: East Carolina University.

CHAPTER FIVE

District Curricula

Too many principals take a passive, hands-off stance with respect to the district curricula, falsely assuming that the district guides are of little consequence to them. The truth of the matter is that district curricula, if effectively conceptualized and implemented, can significantly affect the daily acts of teaching and learning. District curricula, therefore, must become the business of school principals. This chapter describes briefly each of the district's tasks and then explains how principals can exercise their influence on district curricula. It should be noted that in the case of charter schools, most are regarded as districts and make their own curriculum decisions in conjunction with their advisory boards. However, when a charter school belongs to an organization that runs several schools, it may not have sole authority over curriculum matters.

From our observations, large districts tend to have established curriculum departments with systematic processes that create materials for systemwide use. In smaller districts, much curriculum work tends to be left to local schools with some guidance from central office, where someone may be designated as the curriculum contact.

DISTRICT FUNCTIONS

The nine functions identified in Chapter 2 are explained here. Keep in mind that the balance between district and school functions should be determined locally.

Develop and Implement Curriculum-Related Policies

Policy making, of course, is the prerogative of the school board. However, in most districts, the board relies on the superintendent to suggest where policies are needed and to frame draft policies that reflect board views. In turn, superintendents look to principals for ideas for improvement. Because policies are critical in providing general direction for the administration of the schools, principals should work through the superintendent to ensure that board policies set a forward-looking direction.

In his design of a curriculum audit (now done mainly through the Phi Delta Kappa's Curriculum Management Center), English (2000) recommends that the board develop policies in the following areas: a planned relationship between the written, the taught, and the tested curricula; test and textbook adoption; and curriculum-related budgeting. In conducting curriculum audits, English now seems to use 5 audit standards and 22 "characteristics" in determining if policies are adequate (see Frase, English, & Posten, 2000). The expanded list includes elements such as curriculum monitoring, staff development, and equal access.

Here is an example of the policy recommended by English and his colleagues in the area of the tested curriculum.

> The district will establish models for determining the effectiveness of instructional programming at district, school, and classroom levels. Evaluations will focus on determining the extent to which students are achieving and maintaining their mastery of appropriate specific learning opportunities and the extent to which instructors are displaying effective conveyance of curriculum in the classrooms. (Vertiz, 1994, p. 286)

Develop a Vision of a Quality Curriculum

We have found it helpful in working with several school districts to assist them in developing a vision of a quality curriculum. The vision becomes a set of guidelines for evaluating all curriculum products. For example, if the vision statement speaks of a curriculum that values diversity, one would expect to see a U.S. history curriculum guide that gives significant attention to the struggle for equity by African Americans. (The process of developing a vision, explained briefly here, is discussed more fully in Chapter 6.) A group process is recommended, with individuals first working on their own and then sharing the results with the rest of the group. Each person lists ten adjectives that characterize the vision of curriculum quality and then expands on each adjective with a sentence or two. Here is an example:

> *Global:* The curriculum helps students understand that all nations are interconnected.

Develop the District's Educational Goals

An educational goal is a broad statement of the outcomes the district wants to achieve for all students throughout the educational program, from kindergarten to grade 12. Here is an example of an educational goal:

- Understand mathematical concepts and apply mathematical skills and knowledge in solving problems.

Although Spady and Marshall (1991) recommend "transformational" outcomes that transcend traditional subjects, several conservative citizen groups have complained that outcomes such as "quality producers" are too value laden and intrude into family responsibilities. As a consequence, most districts that enthusiastically adopted transformational outcomes seem to have backed off, substituting more traditional ones.

Most state frameworks include goal statements. If the district decides to develop its own or add to the state's goals, then principals should have significant input into the process. The process of developing goals is more fully explained in Chapter 6.

Develop a Common Program of Studies for All Students

The program of studies is the collective set of educational experiences offered at a given level of schooling. Thus, a school district typically would have three programs of study—one for elementary, one for middle, and one for high schools. The district should define a common mastery core curriculum for all students and then enable individual schools to go beyond the core curriculum by adding special electives. The program of studies usually includes the following elements:

- Subjects required at each grade level
- Electives offered at the elementary, middle, and high school level
- Recommended time allocations for each subject at each level
- Credits for each subject
- Promotion and graduation requirements

Obviously, the program of studies will reflect state and school board stipulations with respect to graduation requirements.

The decision about the scope and nature of the program of studies is crucial, because it affects student learning, budget, facilities, schedules, and staffing. Principals should therefore use every opportunity to influence the district's decisions with respect to the level of schooling for which principals are responsible. Additional information about developing the school's program of studies is provided in Chapter 7.

Develop Documents for the Specific Subject

The previous documents have applied to the entire program of studies—all subjects at all levels. District leaders also need to develop plans and processes for developing scope and sequence charts and curriculum guides for individual subjects. A detailed explanation of the process can be found in Glatthorn's work (1994). Although processes will vary by district, leaders should keep in mind the following eight guidelines, which have been derived from our experience in working with numerous school districts:

1. Review state frameworks to ensure that district products are compatible.

2. Review the curriculum standards recommended by professional groups.

3. Provide in-depth staff development to inform teachers of standards and trends.

4. Involve informed teachers in recommending benchmarks for their grade level. As explained previously, a benchmark is a

more specific component of a standard that is usually assigned to a grade or a grade level. Here are examples from Kendall and Marzano (2007):

U.S. history standard: Understands family life now and in the past.

Benchmark, grades 9–12: Understands how interpretations of Columbus's voyages and his interactions with indigenous peoples have changed over time.

5. Focus on mastery objectives—those that require explicit teaching, careful structuring, and systematic assessment.

6. Keep the scope of the mastery curriculum limited so that classroom teachers can enrich the district mastery curriculum.

7. Develop curriculum guides based on the scope and sequence chart.

8. Ensure that all materials are teacher-friendly—that they are focused on mastery and easy to use.

Select Instructional Materials to Support Curriculum

Only after the mastery curriculum has been developed should the district evaluate and select the instructional materials—the texts, the software, and other media. Even though some districts reverse the process (purchasing basic texts and then developing curriculum from them), the text should serve the curriculum and not drive it. While textbooks provide a glimpse of the basic core of material that may be covered in the curriculum, textbooks in general are not reliable foundations for curriculum. Because textbooks are mass produced and mass marketed, they are not customized to the users' specific goals and needs.

Those arguing for a broader approach beyond textbooks say that our current textbook model sends two distinct messages: to students, this is all you need to know; to teachers, this is all you need to teach. Textbooks are not the curriculum; they are tools, whereas standards drive the curriculum.

In the paradigm shift towards focusing on how students learn versus how we teach, the role, function, and even the format of textbooks are changing, with electronic versions emerging.

Textbooks are not in the place of primacy they once occupied, and they may no longer be the gatekeepers of knowledge. In this digital age, the instructional shift is towards learners using technology and having a multisensory experience by combining audio, video, text, and graphics. With technology, learners can access the information they want when they want it, all through hypertext (Educational Cyber Playground, 2007). Using the textbook as the main driver of curriculum may result in a curriculum gap and inadequate alignment with state assessments, resulting in lower student achievement.

Principals should exercise their influence to ensure that the district's selection process is systematic and objective. As suggested earlier, the primary criterion is that the text and other materials correspond closely with the district curriculum guide and state standards. One simple way of doing this is to note for each objective the specific page numbers in the text or program that relate to that objective. If there is a close fit, then the selection committee can consider other criteria, such as readability, cost, durability, and freedom from bias. A more complex process, curriculum alignment, can also be used. (This process is explained in Chapter 10.) The degree of alignment of textbooks, software programs, and curriculum materials to the state and district curriculum and standards has become the litmus test for the selection of materials. Education vendors market their materials being careful to state that their products are aligned to the various state standards and may provide spreadsheets as proof.

Develop District Curriculum-Based Assessments

Once the curriculum guide has been developed and materials have been selected, the district testing office should proceed to develop the district testing program. This should supplement, not duplicate, the state testing program. Even before the emergence of NCLB and its emphasis on annual increases in test scores, many school districts had established offices or departments focusing on testing and accountability. The functions of the testing office may include disaggregation of test data, development of varied assessments, creation of district benchmark tests and test banks, and general test administration and scoring.

Principals should exercise leadership in ensuring that the district testing program meets the following standards:

- Does not demand excessive time from administrators, teachers, and students.
- Does not require excessive funds for development, administration, and scoring of tests.
- Gives educators and parents important information about student achievement.
- Provides results in a form that teachers can use and understand.
- Uses authentic measures wherever feasible, without relying excessively on paper-and-pencil measures.

Several leaders in the field of assessment have expressed concerns about the excessive and inappropriate use of tests. Darling-Hammond (1990, 2002) and James Popham (2001) raise these concerns about standardized achievement tests: (a) they overemphasize lower-order skills; (b) they exert subtle pressure on teachers to focus on fragmented skills, minimizing teacher creativity; (c) the tasks of preparing for, administering, and recording the results of such tests take away time for "real teaching"; and (d) the results are misused by administrators. Principals should keep these concerns in mind as they evaluate and attempt to influence the district testing program.

Provide Resources Needed by the Schools

The district should implement processes that ensure that each school has the resources it needs to implement curriculum effectively. Those resources include funds, personnel, training, and technical assistance. It is especially important that the district budgeting process results in equity among schools so that all schools have sufficient funds.

Evaluate the Curriculum

The district should have in place a sound plan for evaluating the curriculum.

Documents such as the vision statement and the list of educational goals should be reviewed by the school board, central office staff, school administrators, and school faculties before they are finalized.

Three other evaluations are critical. First, each curriculum guide should be evaluated once it has been completed. Table 5.1 lists criteria that can be used in evaluating the guide. Second, the district should use a pilot test to evaluate how the new guide actually works in practice. Some districts use the first year of implementation as a pilot test. Other districts identify a representative sample of classrooms to test the new curriculum before it is widely disseminated. Regardless of the method used, teachers should have an opportunity to try out the new curriculum and give developers feedback about its effectiveness in the classroom.

Finally, the new curriculum should be evaluated during the first year of full implementation. Teachers should be surveyed about their perceptions of the new curriculum. In addition, student achievement should be monitored closely during that crucial first year.

Exercising Influence as the Principal

Principals can exercise their influence in several ways. First, it is recommended that principals be represented on the district curriculum planning council, which develops and monitors a comprehensive plan for developing curriculum guides for all subjects. Second, principals should be included on every subject matter task force. The task force is the group that develops the curriculum guide for a given subject. Finally, principals should use their informal contacts with district administrators, supervisors, and classroom teachers to influence the direction of curriculum development in their districts. While time constraints may inhibit a principal's active involvement in the curriculum process for all subjects, this is a high-value activity and worth the investment of time. The deep curriculum knowledge from these meetings will be helpful for monitoring and continuous improvement. Once the principal has had input to the initial curriculum development process, then in a time crunch, others may represent the principal at later meetings, providing they give good feedback to keep the principal in the loop.

TABLE 5.1

Criteria for Evaluating Curriculum Guides or Courses

Format and Style

- The guide is formatted and organized so that it is easy to use and to update; the guide is flexible and teacher-friendly.
- The writing and the appearance of the guide are of high professional quality.

Relationship With Other Sources

- The content of the guide reflects the best current thinking about that subject, as exhibited by both sound research and in the standards developed by professional organizations.
- The content of the guide reflects state curriculum standards and state tests.

Focus

- The guide focuses on a limited number of key objectives, resulting in greater depth and providing opportunities for teacher enrichment.

Sequence and Placement

- The grade placement of objectives is developmentally appropriate.
- The grade placement of objectives reflects systematic development and coordination from grade to grade without excessive repetition.
- The grade placement of objectives in one subject is articulated with the placement of objectives in related subjects (e.g., the mathematics guide emphasizes the math needed for successful performance in science at a given grade level).

Content

- The guide reflects an appropriate recognition of the diversity of this society.
- The guide facilitates but does not mandate the integration of content from other subjects.

District staff and teachers will pay greater attention to the principal's curriculum views if the principal is seen as knowledgeable and informed. It is important that principals are seen as having more than a cursory knowledge of curriculum issues. One useful source here is the work edited by Glatthorn (1995), which includes a chapter on the content of each of the subjects in the curriculum (see also Glatthorn, Boschee, & Whitehead, 2006).

CHAPTER SUMMARY

This chapter focuses on district-level responsibilities, including the district's curriculum functions, vision of a quality curriculum, curriculum goals, program of studies and subject documents, development of district curriculum documents, selection of curriculum materials, allocation of resources needed by schools, development of assessments, and evaluation of the curriculum. As part of the leadership role, the principal needs to engage with the district and influence what happens at the district level through intentionality rather than simply resigning himself or herself to whatever originates from the district office. Curriculum making is a coconstructed process between districts and schools, and it is a high-value activity into which the principal, as curriculum leader, must extend strong influence. In Part III, attention is given to principal leadership of curriculum at the school level.

REFERENCES

Darling-Hammond, L. (1990). Achieving our goals: Superficial or structural reforms? *Phi Delta Kappan, 72,* 286–295.

Darling-Hammond, L. (2002). What's at stake in high-stakes testing? *Brown University, Child & Adolescent Behavior Letter, 18*(1), 1–3.

Educational Cyber Playground. (2007). *Technology as media.* Retrieved October 10, 2007, from www.edu-cyberpg.com/NCFR/techmedia.html

English, F. W. (2000). *Deciding what to teach and test: Developing, aligning, and auditing the curriculum.* Thousand Oaks, CA: Corwin Press.

Frase, L. E., English, F., & Posten, W. K., Jr. (Eds.). (2000). *The curriculum management audit: Improving school quality.* Lanham, MD: The Scarecrow.

Glatthorn, A. A. (1994). *Developing the quality curriculum.* Alexandria, VA: Association for Supervision and Curriculum Development.

Glatthorn, A. A. (1995). *The content of the curriculum* (2nd ed.). Alexandria, VA: Association for Supervision and Curriculum Development.

Glatthorn, A. A., Boschee, F., & Whitehead, B. M. (2006). *Curriculum leadership: Development and implementation.* Thousand Oaks, CA: Sage Publications.

Kendall, J. S., & Marzano, R. J. (2007). *Content knowledge: A compendium of standards and benchmarks for K–12 education* (4th ed.). Retrieved October 9, 2007, from www.mcrel.org/standards-benchmarks

Popham, W. J. (2001). *The truth about testing.* Alexandria, VA: Association for Supervision and Curriculum Development.

Spady, W. G., & Marshall, K. J. (1991). Beyond traditional outcome-based education. *Educational Leadership, 49*(2), 67–72.

Vertiz, V. C. (1994). *A curriculum management audit.* Arlington, VA: American Association of School Administrators, National Curriculum Audit Center.

PART III

Providing Leadership

CHAPTER SIX

Developing Vision and Goals

I n this and the next five chapters, the focus now changes from the district's curriculum to the school's curriculum. This chapter suggests processes by which the school can develop its own curriculum vision and goals. These foundation documents can be very useful at the school level. They provide a unifying focus for the faculty. They give a clear sense of direction for curriculum work and instruction by providing a common language. They provide a basis for evaluating curricula. And they provide the occasion for professional dialogue.

DEVELOPING THE SCHOOL'S VISION OF A QUALITY CURRICULUM

If the district has developed its own vision of a quality curriculum, the school faculty, under the direction of the principal, can simply build on and supplement the district vision. The district curriculum should be viewed as the floor, however, not the ceiling. Development of the school-level curriculum is a collaborative process. As a minimum, the school should aim to match its vision with the district vision for curriculum for elementary schools, middle schools, or high schools, as appropriate. To facilitate the process, the school may use any of its professional learning community or subgroup structures, such as correlate teams, quality improvement teams,

Comer teams, whole-faculty study groups, or whatever formation is used at the school level.

The easiest way to accomplish this task is for the faculty to meet in small groups to answer this question: What features should make the curriculum of our school unique? Each group should attempt to identify three adjectives that capture the specialness of the school's curriculum. The principal can then synthesize the results from each group, identifying six factors most frequently mentioned by the small groups. Each group should then discuss the six factors. Following that discussion, each individual should identify no more than three of those six factors that he or she considers essential for the school's vision. The principal meets with a committee of teachers, using the results to draft a tentative version of the school's vision. The draft is then reviewed by the faculty.

Here is an example that a middle school with a technology emphasis developed:

> We endorse the district's vision of a quality curriculum. In addition, we note these features that we especially hope to embody in our curriculum:
>
> > *Developmentally appropriate.* Because the middle school years are especially important in the cognitive development of young adolescents, we envision a curriculum that gives special attention to the developmental nature of learning.
> >
> > *Technologically sophisticated.* As a magnet school emphasizing the educational uses of technology, we envision a curriculum that enables all students to master the technology and to develop a critical perspective about its use.

If the district has not developed its own vision, then the school can use the following, more complex process. (This same process can be used by district leaders who wish to develop a curriculum vision.)

1. Assemble participants and organize them into groups of six. The participants can include parents, students, and educators.

2. Explain the importance of the vision-making process, stressing its future use in shaping and evaluating curriculum products.

3. Develop the knowledge base for the group by reviewing elements such as a changing society; the characteristics of the community; the nature of the student body; and research on curriculum, teaching, and learning.

4. Explain to the participants that they individually should complete this statement: "I have a dream of a curriculum that is . . ." Without any group discussion, each person should complete the statement by writing ten adjectives that capture the essence of his or her vision. Here are some examples: *integrated, meaningful, global, technological, goal oriented.*

5. Each person then jots down a sentence or two expanding on the adjective, as in this example:

   Meaningful: The curriculum should enable the student to find meaning and purpose in what is being studied; the curriculum should connect with the lives of the learners.

6. The members of each group then share their adjectives and sentences with each other, in round-robin fashion, with the group leader listing just the adjectives on the board.

7. Group members can then ask questions of clarification. Members clarify the meaning of the adjectives by reading their expanding sentences again and explaining any ideas that are unclear.

8. Each person then has three minutes to advocate for one of the adjectives. After the advocacy, each member allocates 15 votes to any of the adjectives listed on the board that he or she believes are important.

9. The group discusses further the entire list to be sure that the adjectives with the largest number of votes are those they support most of all.

10. Each group presents its results to the larger group, and the facilitator of the session helps to identify commonalities and find a consensus.

An example of a curriculum vision is shown in Table 6.1.

The process explained here is our version of the nominal group process, which attempts to capture the advantages of both individual

TABLE 6.1

Example of a District Vision of Curriculum

We have a dream of a curriculum of excellence that is . . .

1. *Meaningful:* Emphasis on active construction of meaning helps students find purpose in their studies.

2. *Technological:* The curriculum uses technology, examines the influence of technology on students' lives, and gives students useful technological skills.

3. *Socially responsible:* Students develop social responsibility and citizenship participation in a democracy and are sensitive to the needs of the disadvantaged and the aged.

4. *Multicultural:* The curriculum reflects community and national cultural diversity so students develop a sense of pride in their own heritage and a respect for that of others.

5. *Reflective:* The curriculum fosters in students the skills and attitudes of reflection so that they are able to think critically, creatively, and affirmatively.

6. *Holistic:* Emphasis is on all aspects of growth and all types of human intelligence.

7. *Global:* The curriculum develops in students an awareness of global interdependence in all aspects of life, including environment and the economy.

8. *Open-ended:* The curriculum is open to revision and continued refinement, and it provides open access to all students so that students are not tracked into dead-end careers.

9. *Outcomes based:* Students develop the critical skills and acquire the knowledge they need for effective lifelong learning in a changing society.

and group thinking. Further information about the nominal group process can be found in Dewey (2007).

This version of the vision should be seen as an initial tentative framing of desirable characteristics to be reviewed by all constituencies, including the school board. Once the vision has been developed, the principal should ask the faculty to review it from time to time to ensure that it still represents their ideals. As Fullan (2007) notes, vision building is an interactive, ongoing process, not a one-time event.

Some cautions about vision building should be noted. First, the visioning process need not come first in school improvement. Some research suggests that in schools that are improving, the principal and faculty focus on solving problems. After solving several problems, they become aware of an evolving vision. In this process, the vision emerges from practice. Second, the vision-building process should not become a meaningless exercise. The principal needs to stress the importance of the process. Finally, the vision should be used to guide all the key aspects of the curriculum-making process.

DEVELOPING THE SCHOOL'S CURRICULUM GOALS

Two goal-related tasks are important in developing the school's curriculum: (a) identifying the educational goals and (b) aligning goals with programs and subjects.

Identifying the Educational Goals

If the district has developed its own goal statement, the school can simply add any goals it considers essential for its program. If goals do not presently exist, the principal can lead the faculty in using either an inductive or deductive process.

In using either the inductive or the deductive process, leaders should check state standards as a source of educational goals. Usually, a group of subject standards can suggest a goal.

Using the Inductive Process

In using the inductive process, the principal first identifies the educational programs that exist in the school. In most schools, three programs make a contribution: the activities program, the student services program, and the curriculum program. Schools that require students to participate in volunteer work would add the volunteer program; those that have extensive apprenticeships or mentorships would include those as well.

The process begins by asking the faculty responsible for each of the noncurricular programs to identify their goals. Here, for example, is a goal for the activities program:

Students will develop the skills and knowledge needed for effective leadership.

Even though most of these programs operate without explicit goals, the goal statement is useful in several ways: it provides a focus for faculty efforts, it provides a basis for evaluation, and it provides a rationale for continuance.

The other part of the inductive process is for each subject matter team (or for special committees structured around the subjects) to identify the goals for that subject. Here is an example of a goal for science:

Students will become competent in the field of science, developing an understanding of scientific concepts, acquiring scientific curiosity, valuing science as a way of knowing, and using knowledge to solve scientific problems.

The separate goal statements are then combined and reviewed in their entirety by the faculty. The inductive process is based on the commonsense understanding that these programs exist, that they will continue to exist, and that they have implicit goals that need only be made explicit. The inductive process is simpler than the deductive one explained next; its chief limitation is that it may serve simply to maintain the status quo. It also runs the risk of ignoring important curriculum goals that transcend traditional subjects, such as "develop learning skills."

Using the Deductive Process

In using the deductive process, the faculty members wipe the slate clean and take a completely fresh look at what they are trying to achieve. In most instances, they invite parents, older students, and other citizens to join them in the process. Usually the process follows this sequence.

1. The principal orients the group to the importance and nature of their task, emphasizing that they will identify the broad

educational goals for the entire educational experience—all programs, all grades.

2. The principal helps the group develop the needed knowledge base, reviewing information such as the following: the changing nature of society; the shape of the future; the nature of the community; the special characteristics of the student body; and current research on curriculum, teaching, and learning.

3. The participants review goal statements developed by professional organizations (such as the Association for Supervision and Curriculum Development), by their own state and other states, and by other school systems. An excellent source of goal statements is Goodlad (2004). The list developed by Goodlad seems to be a comprehensive one that could easily be modified for current use. The group should also find it helpful to review the state standards.

4. With the principal playing an active role, the participants decide on the general issues that will affect their work: Will the goal statement emphasize the subjects in the curriculum or transcend those subjects? How specific should the goal statement be? What format should be used?

5. With these matters resolved, each group develops its own tentative list of goals.

6. The several statements are synthesized into one comprehensive list that is reviewed, systematized, and organized so that it is clear, coherent, and nonredundant.

7. The final list is presented to stakeholders in accordance with the district's process, usually to the superintendent and then to the school board.

Examples of some goals for a middle school are shown in Table 6.2.

Aligning Goals With Programs and Subjects

If the deductive process has been used, the educational goals need to be aligned with the school's educational programs, and the curriculum goals then need to be assigned to the individual subjects.

TABLE 6.2

Some Examples of Educational Goals for Middle School Learners

Learning Skills

- Read with understanding, reason logically, and think critically.
- Write clearly and effectively and use writing as a way to learn.
- Learn creative thinking, problem solving, and expression in a variety of media.
- Speak and listen well, especially in structured situations.
- Use the computer to solve problems, compose, and process information.
- Learn important concepts and the special skills of English language, literature, mathematics, science, foreign language, social studies, and the arts.
- Understand the nature and importance of physical and mental health.

Personal Skills and Attitudes

- Cope with changes in family, community, and society.
- Make sound, moral decisions, including decisions about careers, work, finances, use of media, and other important personal issues.
- Value own ethnic identity and treat others with respect, regardless of age, gender, class, or ethnic origin.
- Develop attitudes of responsible citizenship and working cooperatively with others.
- Develop an awareness of global interdependence.

Once the comprehensive set of educational goals has been developed, a committee led by the principal needs to allocate the educational goals to the programs offered in the school. A form similar to the one shown in Table 6.3 is useful here. Note that it lists across the top the three basic educational programs—the curriculum, the activities program, and the student services program (including guidance and health). The goals are listed down the left-hand side. The committee considers each goal to determine which program should be primarily responsible for, and which should contribute to, the accomplishment of that goal.

TABLE 6.3

Analyzing Educational Goals

Directions: For each educational goal listed, indicate which program should be primarily responsible by putting the letter *R* in the appropriate cell. Then indicate which other programs should contribute by using the letter *C*.

Educational Goal	Curriculum Program	Activity Program	Student Services Program
1. Become a good citizen	R	C	
2.			

NOTE: To conserve space, only one goal is shown here.

Once the general curriculum goals have been identified, they must be allocated to the several subjects. In this process, a matrix listing the curriculum goals down the left-hand side and the subjects across the top can be helpful. Respondents use the same symbols explained in Table 6.3 (*R* for "primarily responsible"; *C* for "contribute"). An example is shown in Table 6.4. Each teacher should complete the form, with an administrative assistant compiling the results. The results are then discussed in a faculty meeting to ensure that each goal is emphasized in at least one subject and reinforced in others.

By means of these goal-related tasks, the faculty members working together have produced the following:

- A list of broad educational goals for the entire educational program
- A list of goals for the activity program, which can be used to give direction to that program
- A list of goals for the student services program, which can provide guidance for that staff
- A set of goals for each subject in the curriculum, which can be used both to develop and evaluate the curriculum

TABLE 6.4

Allocating Curriculum Goals to the Subjects

Directions: For each of the curriculum goals listed below, indicate which subjects you think should be primarily responsible for that goal, using the letter *R*. Then indicate which other subjects should contribute, using the letter *C*.

Curriculum Goals	Arts	English	Math	Science	Social Studies
1. Become a good citizen	R	C		C	R
2.					

NOTE: To conserve space, only one goal is shown here.

Throughout the process, the principal should emphasize its importance. It is not simply a rhetorical exercise; it results in meaningful goals that will be used to develop, evaluate, and improve the entire educational program. The processes explained in this chapter should result in documents that will be useful in the entire curriculum-making process, providing a foundation for all the curriculum work that follows.

CHAPTER SUMMARY

This chapter focuses on the initial stages of principal leadership of the school-level curriculum-making process through the sequence of developing the school's vision of a quality curriculum, developing the school's curriculum goals, and aligning goals with programs and subjects. Practical suggestions are offered for the internal group process, which may be used to facilitate the staff interactions. Once the school's vision is clear, staff can begin to reconceptualize its program of studies, as discussed in the next chapter.

REFERENCES

Dewey, J. (2007, June). *Enhanced group facilitation: Techniques and process.* Paper presented at American Evaluation Association (AEA) & the Centers for Disease Control and Prevention (CDC) 2007 Summer Evaluation Institute, Atlanta, Georgia. Retrieved October 10, 2007, from www.eval.org/SummerInstitute07/Handouts/si07.deweyF.pdf

Fullan, M. G. (2007). *The new meaning of educational change* (4th ed.). New York: Teachers College.

Goodlad, J. I. (2004). *A place called school: Twentieth anniversary edition* (2nd ed.). New York: McGraw-Hill.

CHAPTER SEVEN

Rethinking the Program of Studies

T he statements of the curriculum vision and goals can be very useful in the next important step, developing the school's program of studies. The program of studies is the total set of offerings provided for a group of learners at a particular level of schooling. In developing the program of studies, the principal and the faculty have essentially two choices: (a) renew the program of studies by fine-tuning the existing program to be sure that it is serving the present student body effectively or (b) restructure the program of studies, reconceptualizing the entire curriculum as a completely new program of studies. Both processes are useful when one or more of the following conditions exist:

- The school faces an accrediting review or needs to respond to a curriculum audit
- The student body seems to have changed significantly
- Staff turnover is high
- Student achievement has not improved satisfactorily over the course of a few years, and the school is not meeting its AYP targets under the NCLB mandates or state accountability requirements
- The school is in a school improvement status and under NCLB sanctions

- State Board of Education or district action has introduced new curriculum requirements, curriculum revisions, or changes in assessments
- New leadership creates a climate for change

This chapter explains both the renewing and the restructuring processes.

RENEWING AN EXISTING PROGRAM OF STUDIES

The principal and the faculty should consider renewing the existing program when they believe only minor changes are needed or when resources are limited. The following process has been used successfully by several schools:

1. *Develop the knowledge base.* Organize reliable information about the following: student demographics, student achievement by subgroups, student success at the next level of schooling or in careers, cost of offering each subject, faculty loads, and class size. Also, review current research on curriculum, teaching, and learning. Include electronic/digital learning.

2. *Identify the constraints and resources.* Check state requirements with respect to required subjects, curriculum revisions, grade levels, credits, and time allocations. Analyze the nature of the district's core curriculum. Assess the budgetary and other resources available.

3. *Determine the criteria to be used in evaluating the present program of studies.* The following criteria are suggested (see Glatthorn, 1994, for additional details):
   - *Goal-oriented:* Focuses on goals and enables students to accomplish the district's mastery goals.
   - *Balanced:* Provides an appropriate balance between required and elective subjects.
   - *Integrated:* Emphasizes the interconnectedness of learning while giving appropriate emphasis to the subjects.
   - *Reinforcing of skills:* Reinforces essential skills (such as writing and studying) across the curriculum.

- *Open-ended:* Does not track students into dead-end programs.
- *Responsive:* Responds to the special needs of learners, including the various NCLB subgroups, and to 21st-century learning needs.
- *Productive:* Achieves the results intended.

4. *Use the criteria in designing a comprehensive evaluation.* For each criterion, identify the methods that will be used in gathering data. Here are the methods that can be used:
   - *Survey:* Parents, faculty, students
   - *Interview:* Parents, faculty, students, administrators
   - *Observe:* Classrooms, student activities, other areas
   - *Analyze documents:* Test scores, vision and goal statements, other documents

5. *Systematize data, make final assessments for each criterion, and report results in a public document.* The final report should include the following elements: executive summary, methods used, evaluations for each criterion, and recommendations for action.

6. *Discuss the final report with parents and teachers and prepare a strategy for action.* The strategy for action should include specific steps that will be taken to improve the program of studies. The following strategies might be undertaken:
   - Add a new course, including online courses.
   - Drop an existing course.
   - Modify/redesign existing courses.
   - Change the time and sequence of course taking.
   - Combine two or more courses.
   - Modify requirements and time allocations. Consider double-dosing and looping where appropriate. (Double-dosing is a technique whereby the instructional time is doubled to enable students to accomplish mastery. Looping is when a class of students stays with the same teacher for two or more years or grade levels.)
   - Change the school schedule.
   - Change instructional organization by creating new professional learning community teams and modifying grouping arrangements.

Because all these changes have major implications for student learning, staffing, and budgeting, they should be reviewed by the faculty, discussed with parents and students, and presented to the school board or appropriate body for review. Unless there are urgent state and district mandates or another emergency, the renewal plan should be implemented prior to the start of a new school year instead of such change being attempted midstream during the year.

RESTRUCTURING THE PROGRAM OF STUDIES

As noted earlier, restructuring is a radical process of reconceptualizing and redesigning an entire program of studies for a given level of schooling. Under NCLB, restructuring is an option for schools under school improvement sanctions. At least a year of planning is recommended using a process that develops stakeholder ownership for the restructuring plan. Such radical restructuring efforts typically attempt to accomplish two key redesign goals:

1. Redefine the nature of general education by specifying what all students should know, emphasizing outcomes, not courses and credits.

2. Rethink the way learning experiences should be organized to accomplish those outcomes by ignoring existing subject matter distinctions.

This section reviews current approaches to restructuring and explains a process that schools can use.

Current Approaches

At the time of this writing, there seem to be several current approaches to restructuring programs of study, including the following:

- Sizer's (2004) work with his Coalition of Essential Schools focuses on a smaller range of curricular goals to reduce class size and personalize instruction and learning environments in an atmosphere of trust and high expectations, multiple assessments based on performance of authentic tasks, democratic governance practices, and close partnerships with the school's community.

- America's Choice is a comprehensive reform model that focuses on instruction aligned with standards, extensive professional development, and parent involvement. The program mandates a core curriculum in literacy and mathematics, tutoring for struggling students, and a school leadership team to coordinate implementation (May, Supovitz, & Perda, 2004).
- Gardner's (2000) Multiple Intelligences approach uses the following eight multiple intelligences as redesign concepts: linguistic, musical, logical-mathematical, spatial, bodily-kinesthetic, interpersonal, intrapersonal, and naturalist (see Armstrong, 2000, for practical applications).
- Ways of Knowing emphasizes the essential ways of knowing (aesthetic, scientific, interpersonal, intuitive, narrative, formal, practical, and spiritual). The theory and concepts are well articulated in Eisner (1985, 2004). Several Ways of Knowing curriculum series in math, science, and language arts have emerged.
- The Comer (2004) model emphasizes the decision-making process, parent involvement, and the provision of comprehensive services to the disadvantaged; the curriculum is comprehensive, giving attention to the social, affective, and cognitive development of the child.
- Success for All is designed to ensure success for all children in the beginning years of schooling. Its key features are the following: (a) a reading program that integrates whole language and phonics for 90 minutes each day, (b) homogeneous reading groups, (c) one-to-one tutoring, (d) cooperative learning, and (e) family support services (for research on its effectiveness, see Borman & Hewes, 2002; Chambers, Slavin, Madden, Cheung, & Gifford, 2004).
- Accelerated Schools emphasizes three core principles: unity of purpose, school site empowerment, and building on strengths. The curriculum gives special attention to language in all subjects, providing an early introduction to writing and reading for meaning (see Chasin & Levin, 1995; Siegle, 2006).
- The Copernican Plan (Carroll, 1994) is about reorganizing time to support learning. It is chiefly identified with block scheduling that provides extended periods of time (90 or more minutes) for the intensive study of fewer subjects. Carroll notes as well that such scheduling also includes evaluation

based on mastery credit, individual learning plans, and the dejuvenilizing of high schools. (Also, see Freeman, 2001.)

In addition, mention must be made of other programs of study that involve different approaches to curriculum.

- *International Baccalaureate (IB) Programme with the IB Diploma:* The IB programmes cover primary to high school, with a challenging two-year college preparation curriculum in the IB Diploma Programme aimed at students ages 16 to 19.
- *American Diploma Project (ADP):* In 2008, the ADP Network includes 32 states that are dedicated to making sure every high school graduate is prepared for college or work by raising the rigor of high school standards, assessments, and curriculum and aligning expectations with the demands of postsecondary education and work.
- *Advanced Placement (AP) programs:* The AP program offers college-level courses, allowing students the opportunity to earn credit or advanced standing at most of the nation's colleges and universities.
- *Early College High Schools:* The Early College High Schools, promoted by the Bill and Melinda Gates Foundation, provide a unique opportunity for traditionally underserved students to earn a high school diploma and two years of college credit applicable towards an associate's or a bachelor's degree. The schools' purpose is to increase graduation rates and college-readiness.

Each of these plans has its own advocates who report success with that program. One of the few systematic reviews of the effectiveness of such programs (including Comer, Coalition of Essential Schools, and Success for All) reached several conclusions: (a) most of the programs studied had some research support, (b) these restructuring programs are feasible, (c) none can be made "teacher-proof," and (d) Success for All seems to have the greatest externally developed research support (Herman & Stringfield, 1995).

Perhaps the best advice about choosing a total program is to check its track record. Three sources are very helpful here: Borman and Hewes, 2002; CSR Quality Center, 2005; and Herman et al.,

1999. All three sources are objective, without bias toward any program, and are results oriented, using student growth and achievement as the basic measures.

A Homegrown Process

Schools wishing to develop their own homegrown models of restructuring can use a process similar to the following:

1. As explained in the preceding chapter, identify the general educational goals and the outcomes to be achieved through all program components.

2. Review those educational goals and determine which are the goals of the mastery curriculum. These mastery curriculum goals are the outcomes to be achieved through the structured, planned part of the curriculum.

3. Identify the new organizing structures by which those mastery goals can be achieved. The organizing structures are the new "courses," although it might be better to think of them as the major concepts or themes by which learning is organized. Because this process is highly creative, it is difficult to be formulaic about it. However, following are some approaches that can be used:
   - Review the existing attempts listed earlier to see what can be learned from them.
   - Reflect on the goals and try to find clusters and patterns that link them.
   - Consider existing subjects. It may well be that the best way to understand mathematical concepts and skills is through a course called "Mathematics." However, be alert to new ways by which those old courses might be linked—such as in a course called Technological Systems that would combine science, mathematics, and social studies.
   - Consider the learners—their needs and interests.
   - In thinking about new structures, play with diagrams or schematics.

4. Through a brainstorming process, identify a small number (perhaps three to seven) organizing structures. List them and

note the traditional subjects from which they will draw their content. Here is one example for middle school:

- *Problem solving* (math, science, social studies)
- *Wellness* (health, science, physical education, social studies)
- *Creative studies* (language arts, technology, science, home economics, music, art)
- *Community* (social studies, science, language arts)
- *Communication* (language arts, computer science, science, social studies, art)
- *Special interests* (a range of electives not restricted to subjects)

5. For each organizing structure, identify the model or models of teaching that would probably be most effective (see Joyce, Weil, & Calhoun, 2003, for a full explication of the models).

6. Develop a matrix that shows the relationship between the mastery goals identified and the new structures to ensure that all goals have been emphasized without excessive repetition. Make any modifications necessary.

7. Summarize the results in a large chart that shows the following: the organizing structure, the mastery goals it will be responsible for achieving, the model of teaching it will emphasize, and the percentage of the total program time it will require.

8. Develop a sample weekly schedule showing the new organizing structures, the time allocated, and how they fit into a schedule. Consider using radical new scheduling approaches (such as that proposed by the Copernican plan, discussed in more depth in Chapter 8 under "The Nature of a Learning-Centered Schedule: 5. Providing Flexibility in Using Time"). Developing the sample schedule is a practical test of the feasibility of the program.

9. Develop scope and sequence charts for the new organizing structures. For each organizing structure, identify its strands, the major recurring elements that will be emphasized in each grade level. For each strand and each grade, identify the major outcomes that students will achieve.

10. Use that scope and sequence as the basis for writing the new units of study, lesson plans, and assessments.

Chapter Summary

Both renewing and restructuring the program of studies have their own advantages. Renewing is simpler, takes less time, uses fewer resources, and is less risky for all involved. Restructuring is systemic, comprehensive, and bolder in conception. The principal and faculty need to study each approach carefully before jumping on the current bandwagon. NCLB sanctions, especially for Title I schools, include corrective action and restructuring, incorporating curriculum reforms. The curriculum development process engages the whole school, creates conversations around curriculum design and redesign, and fosters ownership by stakeholders. (See also Wiggins & McTighe, 2007, for the "schooling by design" approach.) In the next chapter, we look at designing a learner centered schedule.

References

Armstrong, T. (2000). *Multiple intelligences in the classroom* (2nd ed.). Alexandria, VA: Association for Supervision and Curriculum Development.

Borman, G. D., & Hewes, G. M. (2002). The long-term effects and cost-effectiveness of Success for All. *Educational Evaluation and Policy Analysis, 24,* 243–266.

Carroll, J. M. (1994). The Copernican plan evaluated: The evolution of a revolution. *Phi Delta Kappan, 76,* 105–113.

Chambers, B., Slavin, R. E., Madden, N. A., Cheung, A., & Gifford, R. (2004). *Effects of Success for All with embedded video on the beginning reading achievement of Hispanic children.* Baltimore, MD: Johns Hopkins University, Center for Research on the Education of Students Placed at Risk.

Chasin, G., & Levin, H. M. (1995). Thomas Edison Accelerated Elementary School. In J. Oakes & K. H. Quartz (Eds.), *Creating new educational communities, schools, and classrooms where all children can be smart.* Chicago: University of Chicago Press.

Comer, J. P. (2004). *Leave no child behind: Preparing today's youth for tomorrow's world.* New Haven, CT: Yale University Press.

Comprehensive School Reform (CSR) Quality Center. (2005). *Moving forward: A guide for implementing comprehensive school reform & improvement strategies.* Retrieved October 11, 2007, from www .csrq.org/documents/MovingForwardGuideFinal 11-09-05.pdf

Eisner, E. (Ed.). (1985). *Learning and teaching the ways of knowing.* Chicago: University of Chicago Press.

Eisner, E. (2004). *The arts and the creation of mind* (new ed.). New Haven, CT: Yale University Press.

Freeman, C. (2001). *Blocking the school schedule: Potential for instructional change.* Retrieved August 24, 2006, from University of Minnesota, College of Education and Human Development, Center for Applied Research and Educational Improvement Web site: http://cehd.umn.edu/ CAREI/Reports/summary.html#BlockSchoolSched

Gardner, H. (2000). *Intelligence reframed: Multiple intelligences for the 21st century.* New York: Basic Books.

Glatthorn, A. A. (1994). *Developing the quality curriculum.* Alexandria, VA: Association for Supervision and Curriculum Development.

Herman, R., Aladjem, D., McMahon, P., Masem, E., Mulligan, I., & O'Malley, A. (1999). *An educator's guide to schoolwide reform.* Washington, DC: American Institutes for Research.

Herman, R., & Stringfield, S. (1995, April). *Ten promising programs for educating disadvantaged students: Evidence of impact.* Paper presented at the annual meeting of the American Educational Research Association, San Francisco.

Joyce, B., Weil, M., & Calhoun, E. (2003). *Models of teaching* (7th ed.). Boston: Allyn & Bacon.

May, H., Supovitz, J. A., & Perda, D. (2004). *A longitudinal study of the impact of America's Choice on student performance in Rochester, New York, 1998–2003.* Retrieved October 2, 2007, from University of Pennsylvania, Graduate School of Education, Consortium for Policy Research in Education Web site: www.cpre.org/images/stories/cpre_ pdfs/AC-10.pdf

Siegle, D. (2006). The last word: An interview with Gene Chasin, CEO of Accelerated Schools Plus. *Journal of Advanced Academics, 18*(1), 146–154.

Sizer, T. R. (2004). *Horace's compromise: The dilemma of the American high school.* New York: Houghton Mifflin.

Wiggins, G., & McTighe, J. (2007). *Schooling by design: Mission, action, and achievement.* Alexandria, VA: Association for Supervision and Curriculum Development.

CHAPTER EIGHT

Committing to a Learning-Centered Schedule

Although many professors of school administration seem to sneer at schedule making as only a minor "technical" skill, it is in fact a crucial aspect of school effectiveness and plays an important role in delivering a quality curriculum. Essentially, the schedule can be seen as the mechanism by which resources are allocated—time, space, and personnel. In a sense, they who control the schedule control the school's resources. This chapter argues for a learning-centered schedule and explains how principals can make the school's schedule more facilitative of student learning and supportive of the curriculum and a crucial element in instructional design and redesign.

THE NATURE OF A LEARNING-CENTERED SCHEDULE

To understand the goal of efforts in this area, it is important to know what constitutes a good schedule. The key attributes are listed in Table 8.1 and discussed below, first in general terms and then more specifically.

The first general observation to note about these attributes is that many of them contradict each other. For example, if the only consideration were to maximize learning time, teachers would have no planning time. If a teachable assignment reflecting teacher

TABLE 8.1

Characteristics of a Learning-Centered Schedule

1. The schedule maximizes instructional time. The schedule reflects curricular priorities and gives first priority to students' learning needs. Administrators and teachers cooperate in defending instructional time.

2. The schedule facilitates the professional growth of teachers so that they have time to plan collaboratively and to cooperate in fostering their professional growth.

3. The schedule reflects grouping practices that do not stigmatize students, give all students access to a quality curriculum, and foster student achievement.

4. The schedule gives teachers a teachable situation. Teachers are assigned to their areas of specialization. Wherever possible, teacher preferences about the number and type of preparations and room assignments are given consideration. Classes are neither too large nor excessively heterogeneous.

5. The schedule is flexible and learning oriented. Time is organized according to learning needs, instead of learning being constrained by rigid time frameworks.

6. The schedule is responsive to the needs of students and teachers, allowing sufficient time for relaxing, eating, and taking care of personal needs.

SOURCE: Anderson (1985), Dempsey & Traverso (1983), and Glatthorn (1986).

preferences is all that matters, many teachers would have homogeneous classes. These contradictions suggest that the schedule-making process is essentially a negotiation of trade-offs that results in the best combination of several compromises.

The second point is that these attributes are operationalized in a somewhat differential manner, depending on school level and type of schedule. Elementary teachers in a self-contained classroom and middle school teachers with a block-of-time schedule can make many of these decisions on their own. High school teachers coping with a complex period schedule face more challenging constraints.

1. Maximizing Instructional Time

In examining the specific issues identified in the table, the first and most important consideration is that the schedule maximizes instructional time and reflects curricular priorities. Noninstructional time, such as study and homeroom periods, is kept to a minimum. Elementary and middle school teachers allocate time to several subjects on the basis of the school's curricular priorities, not their own preferences. This guideline is especially significant for elementary mathematics and science. The research in general suggests that many elementary teachers give relatively little time to those subjects because they feel poorly prepared to teach them.

Once the schedule has been set, time allocations are important also within a subject. Consider, for example, two fifth-grade teachers planning their language arts instruction. One gives a great deal of time to the study of formal grammar and slights the teaching of writing; the other gives no time to the teaching of formal grammar and increases the time given to the teaching of writing. Their students' results reflect the way the teachers have allocated time: the first class learns formal grammar without integrating it into the writing; the second class learns to write, an essential means of communication, but the writing may contain grammatical errors.

Once those allocations have been made, administrators and teachers should cooperate in defending instructional time. They make an explicit contract with each other to keep to an absolute minimum intrusive behaviors, such as calling students from a class, shortening classes because of special assemblies, dismissing students early for extracurricular activities, and interrupting classes with messages and announcements. Though teachers often blame administrators for such practices, many teachers seem to operate on this principle: "No class intrusions—except when I want them."

2. Facilitating Professional Growth

The second characteristic is almost as important as the first. To become truly professional as collaborative leaders, teachers need increased time for planning and professional growth. Johnson (2006) points out that in many schools, the schedule is made without reference to teachers' professional growth needs or the school's need for collaborative planning for school improvement. A recent study of teachers' working conditions (Hirsch & Emerick, 2006) concluded that 94 percent of elementary educators receive less than an hour per day that could be used for planning. Of middle school and high school teachers, 62 percent and 57 percent, respectively, received this time. In the most effective schools, special time is provided so that teachers can plan collaboratively, implement peer coaching programs, undertake action research, participate in professional learning communities, and collaborate with the principal in school improvement programs.

Such special time is provided in several ways. Teacher aides and volunteers can take over classes. Classes can be combined for special assembly programs. The principal and the assistant principal can substitute for teachers. And from time to time, half-day substitutes can be used to provide longer periods of time for staff development and collaborative planning. Obviously, all these compromises take teachers away from their students, but the payoff seems to be worth the sacrifice.

3. Reflecting Healthy Grouping Practices

The way students are grouped for learning is also a critical matter. Because the issue has been so often oversimplified and distorted, it makes sense to clarify three related terms before recommending solutions.

Tracking is assigning students to a stratified sequence of courses with a particular post–high school focus, such as general, vocational, or college preparatory.

Between-class grouping is assigning students to a particular class on the basis of the student's achievement in that subject. Thus, a school might have three levels of mathematics to which students are assigned depending on their ability in mathematics.

Within-class grouping is a process by which a teacher groups students within a class for certain instructional purposes. For example, most elementary teachers divide their classes into three reading groups.

Although many educators are inclined to make the sweeping generalization that "ability grouping is completely wrong," a closer look at the research and the realities of teaching suggest the issue is more complex than it might seem. Table 8.2 presents a summary of that research. The National Forum to Accelerate Middle-Grades Reform (2001), in advocating for open and fair student assignment

TABLE 8.2

Summary of the Research on Ability Grouping

- Curriculum tracking has several serious weaknesses. It results in the stratification of the student body on the basis of social class. It often results in the delivery of an impoverished curriculum to students in low-ability tracks. In most tracking systems, there is little student mobility (Hallinan, 2004).
- Ability grouping for the gifted seems effective, especially if it results in an accelerated curriculum (Brody & Reis, 2004).
- In a classroom in which competition is emphasized, the presence of students perceived as having low ability is a source of motivation for high-ability students; however, the presence of high-ability students decreases motivation for low-ability students (Marcus & Johnson, 2007).
- Classes of extreme heterogeneity pose special problems for teachers; the teacher often has more difficulty managing such classes and individualizing instruction for the students within them (Adams-Beyers, Whitsell, & Moon, 2004).
- In general, heterogeneous between-class grouping seems to achieve better cognitive and affective results for most students (Slavin, 1989).
- Within-class grouping seems most effective in teaching mathematics. However, in teaching beginning reading, some form of the Joplin plan (where students are reassigned on the basis of reading ability) seems most effective (Neumeister & Holmes, 2006).

practices, advises that when students are grouped and regrouped for purposes of instruction, the assignment should be temporary and based on diagnosed needs, interests, and talents of students, not on a single achievement test. Thus, teachers should constantly assess student progress through rigorous and varied methods and make reassignments as appropriate.

School systems that are trying to find the best answer to a very complicated problem have arrived at several compromise solutions. First, they minimize tracking in high school, providing only two tracks: academic and tech-prep. The tech-prep program emphasizes a high-quality curriculum in the core subjects along with technical education for students who aspire to such careers. Second, they provide an accelerated curriculum for the most gifted students, who are grouped for special instruction. While they use heterogeneous grouping as a basis for assigning students to classes, they attempt to reduce the range of abilities in any given class.

This set of decisions should not be seen as necessarily the best answer to this complex problem. It suggests, instead, that faculties need to study the problem very carefully and work out a solution that results in better achievement without stigmatizing students who are deficient in verbal or mathematical abilities.

4. Providing a Teachable Situation

Teachers also need a teachable situation. A teachable situation includes the following elements: class size is manageable; the ability range is not too extreme; teachers are teaching in the area for which they have prepared; teachers have access to good facilities, materials, and equipment; and students are not disruptive. The data suggest that the profession is far from achieving that desired state. Here are some selected findings from a study by Metropolitan Life Insurance (2006):

- One-quarter of teachers (26 percent) report that the equipment in their schools does not meet the needs of students.
- Two in ten teachers (19 percent) do not have enough current textbooks for students.
- Two in ten teachers (18 percent) work where school buildings and grounds are not clean and in good condition.
- Teachers who expect to leave the profession (25 percent) are more likely than others to feel unprepared to maintain order and discipline.
- One in five (20 percent) first-year teachers say that they were not prepared to maintain order and discipline in the classroom.

Obviously, many of these conditions result from starved school district budgets—a situation that is not easily changed. However, principals should continue to lobby professionally for increased funding.

5. Providing Flexibility in Using Time

The fifth guideline involves the flexible use of time. The best schedules serve the requirements of the teaching/learning transaction.

Unfortunately, in most schools, learning is controlled by the schedule. In this sense, the elementary teacher in the self-contained classroom has the most desirable schedule. Teams of middle school teachers who are assigned a block of time also have the advantage of flexible scheduling. It is high school teachers who suffer the most here. If educators wanted to devise the worst possible schedule for learning, they probably would propose the standard high school schedule: 45 minutes a day for all subjects with an occasional double period.

The difficulties of teaching in a rigid 45-minute schedule led the Commission on Restructuring the American High School to recommend strongly that high schools develop more flexible schedules (Dyer, 2003). Dissatisfaction with the status quo has led many high schools to experiment with flexible arrangements, such as the following:

- *Modular schedules:* The schedule is built on short time increments, such as 15-minute modules.
- *Block-of-time schedules:* A team of teachers is assigned a long block of time to divide as they see fit. This includes the 4 × 4 block schedule—four 90-minute, 1-credit classes each semester over four years; the A/B block schedule—four 90-minute, 1-credit classes meeting every other day ("A" days) for an entire school year and four completely different 90-minute, 1-credit classes meeting on alternate days ("B" days) for an entire year; the combination block schedule—a combination of 4 × 4 and A/B block schedules; and the flexible schedule—a combination of 4 × 4 and A/B block schedules but with class length varying from day to day.
- *Rotating period schedules:* A class that meets first period on Monday would meet second period on Tuesday, and so on.
- *The six-day cycle:* The schedule is rotated every sixth day instead of on a weekly basis.

Kussin (2007) and Merenbloom & Kalina (2006) are excellent resources for more information about scheduling alternatives.

Whereas such schedules may seem only to tinker with the standard schedule, a more radical approach has been offered in the Copernican Plan, devised by Carroll (1990). The Copernican Plan provides long blocks of time for intensive study. In one version of the plan, a student would study only two subjects at a time—one in the morning and one in the afternoon—for a 12-week period. Although the plan was initiated with great fanfare in the district where Carroll served as superintendent, full implementation of the plan was impeded by a lack of board support. He summarizes the evidence supporting the effectiveness of this plan in his 1994 article.

Current modifications of the Copernican Plan use such varied terms as *block of time, extended period,* and *90-minute schedules.* Besides equaling traditional schedules in facilitating student learning, they have several other advantages. They reduce the number of preparations for teachers, and they provide extended time for teacher development and team planning. They also enable students to concentrate on a few subjects at a time.

However, several drawbacks can be noted. Anecdotal reports by several principals indicate that many teachers are not taking advantage of the extended period. Their pattern is this: teacher talk for 45 minutes; seat work for 45. Training in "teaching to the block" and training in differentiated strategies are required. Also, the complaints of teachers who believe that students need to learn a subject (such as world languages) over a ten-month sweep have led principals to make several variations on the standard block of time.

6. Responding to Personal Needs

The final guideline is a commonsense reminder that students and teachers are ordinary human beings who need time to relax, eat, and take care of personal needs. In the desire to increase instructional time, some schools have unwisely ignored these needs by reducing the length of the lunch period, cutting back on recess time, and requiring teachers to give up their planning periods to "cover" for teachers who must leave early or attend some other activity.

DEVELOPING A LEARNING-CENTERED SCHEDULE

How can the principal and faculty work toward developing a schedule that is more learning centered? The first part of this section examines first what they can do together and then what teachers, with principal leadership, can accomplish on their own.

Collective Action for Learning-Centered Schedules

The first need is for an organizational structure for accomplishing the goals of schedule revision—either an existing committee or a special task force. The first job of the committee or task force would be to identify the constraints in which they must work; such limits are typically set by the state and the local school board in specifying the minimum number of instructional hours for all schooling; the subjects to be offered; and, in many cases, the minimum number of hours for each subject.

The task force should then review the research cited here, as well as other sources, to build their knowledge base. Ordinarily, it is wise to summarize the knowledge base in a two- or three-page handout and distribute it to all teachers.

With those jobs accomplished, the task force should examine the following issues, usually in the order listed:

1. *How shall we organize the program of studies, grade by grade?* The program of studies, as explained in the previous chapter, is the total set of educational offerings for a given group of students. Answering this question necessitates resolving several specific issues such as (a) what subjects will be required, (b) which elective offerings will be made available, (c) how much curriculum integration will be provided, and (d) how much time will be allocated to each subject.

2. *How shall we assign students to this program of studies?* The central question here, of course, is whether students are assigned on a homogeneous or heterogeneous basis. The issue also involves determining whether a mini-school, an alternative program, a school-within-a-school, academies, or other similar approaches will be used to divide larger schools into smaller units.

   This issue also involves the vexing question of class size. It makes sense to give teams of teachers throughout the school the responsibility of providing instruction to approximately the same number of students, and they should be able to make their own decisions about class size and teacher load. For example, in some schools, it has been possible to give one teacher in a large department or team a sharply reduced teaching schedule simply by increasing average class size by five or six.

3. *By what processes shall we staff for this program of studies?* This question involves matters such as whether teachers work together as teams, how teachers are assigned to subjects and groups of students, and how specialists (such as art, music, foreign language, and physical education teachers) are used. In examining this issue, the committee should keep in mind the special needs of novice teachers. More than anyone else, they need a teachable situation to cope with the demands of the first year in the profession. In too many schools, teacher seniority dictates how teacher preferences are respected; thus, the beginners get the most difficult classes, while the older hands get the easier assignments.

4. *What type of schedule can give the instructional staff the flexibility they need to maximize learning?* At this stage, the task force should examine the scheduling alternatives described above, keeping in mind that the most complicated schedule is not necessarily the best one.

5. *How should time be allocated to the several subjects?* If the school system does not provide guidelines about this issue, the principal and the teachers should develop their own guidelines, ensuring that time allocations reflect curricular priorities. Elementary faculties may wish to consider these recommendations made by Goodlad (2004):

Reading and language arts, 1.5 hours each day

Mathematics, 1 hour each day

Social studies, 2.5 hours each week

Science, 2.5 hours each week

Health and physical education, 2.5 hours each week

Arts, 3.5 hours each week

If teachers decide to integrate reading, language arts, and social studies, they should make the block of time reflect the individual allotments. Middle and high school teachers can consult other current sources that recommend time allotments for those levels.

6. *By what processes can space be allocated for maximum learning?* Space is always in short supply. And in too many instances, decisions about how space is allocated are made on the basis of power and seniority. There is a need instead for professional deliberation about issues such as the following:
   - What are the special space needs of the subjects taught, and how can they best be accommodated?
   - How can we allocate space so that "floating" is minimized?
   - What space can we make available for teacher planning and other professional activities?
   - How can the allocation of space foster collegial interaction?

7. *How can the personal needs of students and teachers and the professional needs of teachers be accommodated?* Here, the committee needs to be especially creative, particularly in finding ways to give teachers extended planning periods. One practical goal would be to provide every teacher with a single planning period on each of four days and two back-to-back planning periods on one day of the week. That double period would be set aside for team planning, with specific guidelines about its use.

Based on their study of these issues, the task force would make recommendations to the entire faculty for their further discussion and modifications.

HOW THE PRINCIPAL AND TEACHERS CAN MAKE MORE EFFECTIVE USE OF THE EXISTING SCHEDULE

Even if the major changes discussed above do not seem feasible, there are still several ways that the principal and the teachers can make more effective use of an existing schedule.

First, the principal can work with teachers to help them allocate time within a particular subject so that it reflects priorities for that subject. One of the best ways to do so is for the teachers to develop yearly schedules and the principal to review them. Chapter 12 explains this process.

With time allocations established for separate subjects and for components of a single subject, teachers need to examine—with the principal's help—how they use time in the classroom. As emphasized in several research reports, time on task is directly related to student achievement (see Silva, 2007). Teachers should also be concerned with the *quality* of learning, not the *quantity*. Instead of being unduly concerned about "How much time on a task?" they should ask as well "What is the quality of the task?"

To understand this distinction more clearly, consider two classes. In Class A, the teacher seems almost obsessed with increasing time on task. He starts class promptly, takes care of business quickly, keeps youngsters busily engaged by close monitoring, makes smooth transitions, and ends just when the bell rings. However, throughout that high-task lesson, the students are working on drill-and-practice materials, emphasizing low-level comprehension of textbook knowledge.

Now in Class B, the teacher is more relaxed. He begins class with a few minutes of talk about last night's basketball game. He seems a bit slow in passing out materials. The transitions are a little rough. And he ends a few minutes early. But throughout the lesson, he has had the students engaged in high-quality learning: they are using knowledge to solve problems, working together cooperatively, and actively communicating with each other.

Class B shows better-quality learning. Here are some signs that indicate quality learning is taking place:

- The students are working hard, and the teacher is facilitating their learning by acting as a cognitive coach, providing the structure they need, modeling, and giving cues. But students are doing most of the work.
- The students are solving problems, using what psychologists call generative knowledge—knowledge that is used and applied. They are minimizing inert knowledge—knowledge that lies fallow because it is not used.
- The students are asking questions. The teacher is stimulating their curiosity, prodding them to ask questions, and rewarding those who do so.
- The students are using language as a means of learning. They are talking in small groups and using writing as a means of learning. The teacher is encouraging and monitoring such use.

- The students are engaged in assessing their learning; they are evaluating their own work and the work of their classmates. The teacher is monitoring these student assessments and adding some, using the assessment process as a means of facilitating learning.
- Finally, and most important of all, the students are learning something significant. When they leave the classroom, they know more than when they entered—about something that matters. That is the crucial task. In assessing the teacher's performance, the observer and the teacher ask, "What did they learn this period that they didn't know when they walked in?"

Next, the principal and teachers can collaborate in defending instructional time. In too many schools, instructional time is reduced by actions such as making public address announcements, summoning students from class, and excusing students for special activities. Whereas teachers are inclined to blame the principal, often the teachers who complain are the same ones who ask to have students excused. Defending instructional time also involves practices such as making announcements through daily staff memos, emphasizing promptness in reporting to class, reducing the incidence of class "cutting," improving student attendance, and reducing passing time between periods.

Finally, the principal and teachers can extend learning time in several ways. They can meet students before school. They can provide remediation after school. And they can give meaningful homework assignments for which students are held accountable.

Obviously, the schedule has a major influence on what students learn. Although not directly affecting the content of learning, a learning-centered schedule can support a quality curriculum.

CHAPTER SUMMARY

Accomplishing a learning-centered schedule is an important function of the principal as curriculum leader. It is best accomplished with active staff input and participation in the decision-making process. A learning-centered schedule protects instructional time as well as providing time for teacher collaboration, interaction, and planning. Scheduling is not a minor clerical task but rather is a planning tool for curriculum and instructional design and redesign to maximize learning outcomes.

REFERENCES

Adams-Byers, J., Whitsell, S. S., & Moon, S. M. (2004). Gifted students' perceptions of the academic and social/emotional effects of homogeneous and heterogeneous grouping. *Gifted Child Quarterly, 48*(1), 7–20. Retrieved October 21, 2007, from http://gcq.sagepub.com/cgi/content/abstract/48/1/7

Anderson, L. W. (1985). Policy implications of research on school time. *School Administrator, 40,* 25–28.

Brody, L. E., & Reis, S. M. (2004). *Essential readings in gifted education series: Vol. 3. Grouping and acceleration practices in gifted education.* Thousand Oaks, CA: Corwin Press and National Association for Gifted Children.

Carroll, J. M. (1990). The Copernican Plan: Restructuring the American high school. *Phi Delta Kappan, 71,* 358–365.

Carroll, J. M. (1994). The Copernican plan evaluated: The evolution of a revolution. *Phi Delta Kappan, 76,* 105–113.

Dempsey, R. A., & Traverso, H. P. (1983). *Scheduling the secondary school.* Reston, VA: National Association of Secondary School Principals.

Dyer, T. J. (2003). *Breaking ranks: Changing an American institution.* Reston, VA: National Association of Secondary School Principals.

Glatthorn, A. A. (1986). How does the school schedule affect the curriculum? In H. J. Walberg & J. W. Keefe (Eds.), *Rethinking reform: The principal's dilemma* (pp. 53–60). Reston, VA: National Association of Secondary School Principals.

Goodlad, J. I. (2004). *A place called school: Twentieth anniversary edition* (2nd ed.). New York: McGraw-Hill.

Hallinan, M. T. (2004, Fall). Whatever happened to the detracking movement: Why children are still grouped by ability. *Education Next, 4*(4). Retrieved October 21, 2007, from www.hoover.org/publications/ednext/3260116.html

Hirsch, E., & Emerick, S. (with Church, K., & Fuller, E.). (2006). *Teacher working conditions are student learning conditions: A report on the 2006 North Carolina teacher working conditions survey.* Chapel Hill, NC: Center for Teaching Quality. Retrieved October 22, 2007, from www.teachingquality.org/pdfs/twcnc2006.pdf

Johnson, S. M. (2006). *The workplace matters: Teacher quality, retention, and effectiveness.* Washington, DC. Retrieved October 10, 2007, from www.nea.org/research/bestpractices/images/wcreport.pdf

Kussin, S. S. (2007). *How to build the master schedule in 10 easy steps: A guide for secondary school administrators.* Thousand Oaks, CA: Corwin Press.

Marcus, L. R., & Johnson, T. (2007). *The future of secondary education: New possibilities for teaching diverse populations in tomorrow's high school.* Retrieved October 21, 2007, from http://horizon.unc.edu/projects/HSJ/Marcus.asp

Merenbloom, E. Y., & Kalina, B. A. (2006). *Making creative schedules work in middle and high schools.* Thousand Oaks, CA: Corwin Press.

Metropolitan Life Insurance. (2006). *The MetLife survey of the American teacher: Expectations and experiences; A survey of teachers, principals and leaders of college education programs.* Retrieved October 22, 2007, from www.metlife.com

National Forum to Accelerate Middle-Grades Reform. (2001). *National Forum Policy Statement: Student assignment in the middle grades; Towards academic success for all students.* Retrieved November 9, 2007, from www.mgforum.org/Policy/abilitygrouping/abilitygrouping.htm

Neumeister, K. L. P., & Holmes, F. (2006). Perfectionism in high-ability students: Relational precursors and influences on achievement motivation. *Gifted Child Quarterly, 50*(3), 238–251. Retrieved October 21, 2007, from http://gcq.sagepub.com/cgi/content/abstract/50/3/238

Silva, E. (2007). *On the clock: Rethinking the way schools use time.* Washington, DC: Education Sector Reports. Retrieved October 10, 2007, from www.educationsector.org/usr_doc/OntheClock.pdf

Slavin, R. E. (1989). Grouping for instruction in the elementary school. In R. E. Slavin (Ed.), *School and classroom organization* (pp. 159–172). Hillsdale, NJ: Lawrence Erlbaum.

CHAPTER NINE

Integrating the Curriculum

One of the unintended consequences of NCLB is the focus on the tested core subjects of reading and math and a lesser focus on science and social studies at the elementary and middle levels. With testing in science under NCLB beginning in 2007, more attention will be placed on science at these levels. At the high school level, the nontested, noncore areas, such as career technical education, have been marginalized, although they have the potential to support the core curriculum if points of convergence are created, especially for reading and writing across the curriculum.

At all levels, teachers tend to address this imbalance by looking for ways to integrate units in other subjects with reading and math. Although there is currently much interest in curriculum integration, some concerns about too much integration have recently been raised. For that reason, it is recommended here that the school faculty, under the leadership of the principal, determine the nature and extent of integration to implement. This chapter reviews the types of curriculum integration, discusses the arguments for and against integration, and suggests a constructive way of resolving the issue.

TYPES OF INTEGRATION

Because the term *integrated curriculum* is used so loosely, it is probably wise to begin with an examination of the types of integration available (for an alternative conceptualization, see Drake, 2007; Fogarty, 2002).

Integrating While Retaining Separate Subjects

There are four ways to integrate the curriculum while maintaining the separate subjects.

1. *Correlation.* The curricula of two related subjects (such as science and mathematics or social studies and English language arts) are developed so that the content of each supports the other. For example, students read Colonial literature in English class while they are studying the Colonial period in social studies.

2. *Skills across the curriculum.* The curriculum can be made more cohesive if developers ensure that skills such as reading, writing, and study skills are reinforced across the curriculum, not confined to English language arts.

3. *Unified curriculum.* The curriculum for a given subject is designed so that the divisions of the subject are minimized and its holistic nature is stressed. Whole language and unified science are examples of unified curricula.

4. *Informal integration.* In this model, the teacher brings in content from one subject while emphasizing the skills and concepts of another. Thus, an elementary teacher teaching a social studies unit on Mexico would informally provide examples of Mexican art and music.

Integrating Two or More Subjects

Most of the current discussion of integration is concerned with the need to combine content from two or more subjects, such as English language arts, social studies, and science. Three major approaches are often used here.

1. *Subject-focused integration.* In this model, the developers begin with one subject (such as social studies) and then combine content from related subjects (such as English language arts and the arts).

2. *Theme focused.* In this model, developers begin by identifying major themes that would be of interest and consequence to students. They then choose content from any subject that supports the theme. For example, a unit on "Conflict and

Violence" might include content from social studies, English language arts, science, and the arts.

3. *Project focused.* In this model, developers identify a complex project that would involve the students, such as developing a model community. In the course of completing such a project, students would need to master skills and concepts from social studies, science, mathematics, the arts, and English language arts.

Other organizing structures can be found in the literature, including the following: world cultures ("Understanding Central America"), aesthetic principles ("Form and Function in the Arts"), minority cultures ("The African American Experience"), and eras of history ("The Industrial Revolution").

ARGUMENTS SUPPORTING INTEGRATION

Several arguments have been advanced supporting the practice of combining two or more separate subjects. First, the research generally supports this type of integration. Vars (1991, 2001) points out that more than 90 studies comparing integrated curricula with traditional curricula have concluded that students learn more through integrated approaches.

Several theoretical arguments are also advanced. Supporters point out that problems in the real world cannot be compartmentalized into one discipline. For instance, solving a problem in water quality would require knowledge of science, mathematics, economics, and political science. They also note that student concerns (such as choosing a career) transcend the disciplines. Finally, they argue that preliminary research on the brain suggests that students learn better when learning is holistic, not fragmented. (See, for example, Beane, 2005; Caine, Caine, McClintic, & Klimek, 2005.)

ARGUMENTS QUESTIONING THE USE OF INTEGRATION

Not all curriculum experts are convinced that integration is totally desirable. Gardner and Boix-Mansilla (1994) are persuasive in arguing for the importance of disciplinary knowledge, noting that students' access to disciplinary knowledge is essential in acquiring a quality education. Their position is supported by Roth's (2000) experience in working with teachers to develop an integrated unit. She concluded that the thematic unit on "1492" resulted in students gaining very superficial knowledge. Other advocates of subject-focused curricula, such as Bruner (2000), note that each discipline has its own way of knowing, its own standards for validating knowledge, and its own key concepts. And Brophy and Alleman (1991) caution that many of the integrated units they have examined were poorly designed collections of activities, only loosely connected.

A PROCESS FOR RESOLVING THE ISSUE

Given the current state of knowledge about curriculum integration, it seems wise for a principal to work with the faculty in deciding how and to what extent they would like to integrate their curriculum. The following steps are recommended:

1. Appoint a curriculum integration task force (or use an existing structure). The essential function of the task force is to develop the school-based model. The group should include the principal, teacher representatives from each teaching team (either grade level or departmental), and a representative of central office staff. The task force would then take all the steps enumerated below.

2. Build the knowledge base: the research on curriculum integration, the research on effective teaching, and the availability of exemplary curriculum materials.

3. Analyze the district curriculum guides to determine to what extent integration seems feasible.

4. Analyze teachers' experience in developing and using integrated curricula, paying special attention to both successes and problems.

5. Examine carefully students' learning needs and community attitudes toward educational innovation.

6. Assess the resources available—especially time, learning materials, and expertise.

7. Study the recommendations offered in Table 9.1. They have been drawn from an analysis of the research and our own

TABLE 9.1

Recommendations for Curriculum Integration

Elementary Schools

- Give primary emphasis to the mastery of the basic skills of reading, writing, and mathematics.
- For the curriculum in beginning reading, use a whole language approach, supplemented by structured teaching of phonics (see Juel, 1991, for the research on this issue).
- For the curriculum in beginning mathematics, focus on that subject but show its applications in science.
- For the science curriculum, focus on scientific understandings but show their application to and relationships with social studies content.
- For the social studies curriculum, encourage the integration of content from the arts.
- In all subjects that are highly verbal in nature, develop curriculum materials that facilitate the learning of reading, writing, and study skills.

Middle Schools

- Give primary emphasis to the study of issues and problems that have developmental significance for middle school learners.
- Continue the emphasis on reading, writing, and study skills in the content areas.
- Develop integrated units that combine English language arts, the arts, and social studies in helping middle school learners deal with issues that are developmentally significant.
- Develop integrated units in science, technology, and health that will provide students with a sound knowledge base in making major behavioral choices.
- Structure the mathematics curriculum so that it continues to emphasize mathematical concepts and skills while showing the applications of mathematics to students' daily lives.
- Ensure that science and mathematics curricula are closely correlated so that students have mastered the mathematical skills required for science.

High Schools

- Give primary emphasis to the mastery of the key concepts and skills of each discipline.
- Continue the emphasis on reading, writing, and study skills across the curriculum.
- Ensure the close correlation of advanced sciences and mathematics.
- Develop an "American Studies" course that thoughtfully integrates American literature, American history, and the arts.

experience. Though based on a solid foundation of knowledge, they should be reviewed carefully for their application to the local context. Note that the recommendations are differentiated according to school level. At the elementary level, teaching the basic skills is the primary responsibility. At the high school level, the individual subjects have greater importance to students facing career and college demands. At the middle school level, freed from the pressure both to teach the basics and emphasize the subjects, the faculty have much greater freedom to innovate.

8. Develop the school's model of integration. To encourage a sense of ownership, emphasize the importance of a grassroots approach that represents teachers' recommendations.

9. Have discussions and develop the appropriate assessments and process for evaluating integrated units with multiple subject content. Include reflection time on what happened during the unit, the success/failure of the unit, and strengths and weakness of the implementation. It is important that the assessments capture the main disciplinary connections and integrating concepts of the unit, not the separate content.

With the school's model selected, each teaching team collaborates in developing the first unit. They implement the unit and evaluate its effectiveness, reporting the results to the task force.

After analyzing the team reports, the task force should modify the model if necessary and develop a long-term calendar for planning and teaching the next five units.

This cyclical process of planning, teaching, evaluating, and revising is likely to result in high-quality units.

CHAPTER SUMMARY

This chapter examines the types of, approaches to, and arguments for and against curriculum integration. The principal leads the process to determine the extent and nature of the desirable integration and involve the staff in such decision making. Curriculum integration does not just evolve; the principal deliberately leads the process as part of curriculum leadership. Schools that implement integration well may find it easier to implement effective curriculum alignment, as addressed in the next chapter.

REFERENCES

Beane, J. A. (2005). *A reason to teach: Creating classrooms of dignity and hope.* Portsmouth, NH: Heinemann.

Brophy, J., & Alleman, J. (1991). A caveat: Curriculum integration isn't always a good idea. *Educational Leadership, 49*(2), 66.

Bruner, J. (2000). *The process of education.* New York: Random House Trade Paperbacks.

Caine, R. N., Caine, G., McClintic, C., & Klimek, K. (2005). *12 brain/mind principles in action: The fieldbook for making connections, teaching and the human brain.* Thousand Oaks, CA: Corwin Press.

Drake, S. M. (2007). *Creating standards-based integrated curriculum: Aligning curriculum, content, assessment, and instruction* (2nd ed.). Thousand Oaks, CA: Corwin Press.

Fogarty, R. (2002). *How to integrate the curricula* (2nd ed.). Thousand Oaks, CA: Corwin Press.

Gardner, H., & Boix-Mansilla, V. (1994). Teaching for understanding in the disciplines—and beyond. *Teachers College Record, 96,* 198–218.

Juel, C. (1991). Beginning reading. In R. Barr, M. L. Kamil, P. B. Mosenthal, & P. D. Pearson (Eds.), *Handbook of Reading Research* (Vol. 2, pp. 759–788). New York: Longman.

Roth, K. J. (2000). Photosynthesis of Columbus: Exploring interdisciplinary curriculum from the students' perspectives. In S. Wineburg & P. Grossman (Eds.), *Interdisciplinary curriculum: Challenges to implementation* (pp. 153–179). New York: Teachers College.

Vars, G. F. (1991). Integrated curriculum in historical perspective. *Educational Leadership, 49*(2), 14–15.

Vars, G. F. (2001). Can curriculum integration survive in an era of high-stakes testing? *Middle School Journal, 33*(2), 7–17.

CHAPTER TEN

Aligning the Curriculum

In the current NCLB-driven era of strong accountability, curriculum alignment has become the base or default setting for teaching and learning. It is seen as a prerequisite step from which instruction and assessment flows. Several different types of curriculum are at work in the school. When they are reasonably congruent with each other, student achievement is improved. This chapter reviews briefly the several types of curriculum and explains how a comprehensive model for aligning these curricula can be planned and executed.

TYPES OF CURRICULA

Seven types of curricula need the attention of the principal.

1. *Recommended curriculum.* The recommended curriculum is that which is recommended by scholars and professional organizations. The best source for the recommendations of professional organizations is Kendall and Marzano (2007).

2. *Written curriculum.* The written curriculum, as the term is used here, is the curriculum that appears in state and locally produced documents, such as state standards, district scope and sequence charts, district curriculum guides, teachers' planning documents, and curriculum units.

3. *Taught curriculum.* The taught curriculum is that which teachers actually deliver day by day.

4. *Supported curriculum.* The supported curriculum includes those resources that support the curriculum—textbooks, software, and other media.

5. *Assessed curriculum.* The assessed curriculum is that which appears in tests and performance measures: state tests, standardized tests, district tests, and teacher-made tests.

6. *Learned curriculum.* The learned curriculum is the bottom-line curriculum—the curriculum that students actually learn.

7. *Hidden curriculum.* This is the unintended curriculum. It defines what students learn from the physical environment, the policies, and the procedures of the school. Here is an example. Each week teachers in an elementary school devote 250 minutes to reading and 50 minutes to art. Students learn this lesson: "In this school, art is not considered very important."

Figure 10.1 shows the relationship of these curricula as they interact with each other. Notice that the research suggests that patterns of influence vary among the several types. The recommended curriculum seems to have little influence on the written, although districts seem to be increasingly concerned with state standards, especially if they are accompanied by state tests. Also, the standards developed by the National Council of Teachers of Mathematics (2000) seem to have had a significant influence in the development of district mathematics guides.

Figure 10.1 Types of Curricula

The written curriculum seems to have a moderate influence on the taught curriculum. Teachers report that they typically check the district guide early in the year, just to remind themselves what it includes. They are much more influenced by the assessed curriculum, especially if they are held accountable for students' results. Students are similarly sensitive to the assessed curriculum, as evidenced in the standard student question, "Is this going to be on the test?"

Teachers are perhaps most sensitive to the learned curriculum, making their decisions on the basis of students' needs, as they perceive them, and students' responses to the taught curriculum. Whereas conventional wisdom holds that teachers are textbook driven, the research suggests that the textbook is only one of several sources that the teacher consults in planning for instruction (see Brown, 1988; Wikimedia Foundation, 2007). Also, textbook series often do not match closely the written curriculum because they are developed for a nationwide mass market. On the other hand, a relationship often exists between the written and the assessed curricula. Typically, the assessment is an objective test that samples low-level learning.

The hidden curriculum has a strong influence on what students learn. Even though students are not always aware of the impact of the hidden curriculum, they experience it every day. For example, an old building with holes in the roof and graffiti on the walls very clearly conveys the message, "People here don't care about this school."

The gaps between curricula have led experts in the field to recommend alignment processes.

English (2000), the chief advocate of alignment, emphasizes the need for a close match between the curriculum and the test. He explains that alignment can be achieved through "frontloading" or "backloading." *Frontloading* means developing the curriculum first and then finding a test to match; *backloading* means developing (or locating) the test first and then developing a curriculum to match (see also English & Steffy, 2001).

We recommend a more comprehensive approach that involves the alignment of all seven curricula. The alignment process is best carried out at the school level. Even though a district or regional approach might be more efficient, the school-based process results in a greater sense of ownership and serves to educate the teachers about the details of the new curriculum guide.

ALIGNING THE RECOMMENDED
AND THE WRITTEN CURRICULA

Aligning the recommended and the written curricula is primarily the responsibility of the task force assigned to develop the curriculum in a given subject area. However, the principal can play a role, as explained below.

The extent to which the recommended curriculum should determine the written curriculum varies from subject to subject. Some professional standards, such as those in mathematics, seem to be well formulated and widely approved; they thus can provide useful guidance for the written curriculum. On the other hand, the standards for English language arts (National Council of Teachers of English and International Reading Association, 1996) have been widely criticized for being too vague and excessively concerned with process; they therefore seem less useful to local developers.

Principals can play an active role in this alignment. If they are members of task forces, they can require the task force to analyze professional and state standards and determine which ones should be used in the district guide. If they are not represented on the task force, they can examine the products to assess whether the recommended curriculum has been given sufficient attention.

ALIGNING THE WRITTEN, THE SUPPORTED,
AND THE ASSESSED CURRICULA

The principal should play an active role in working with teachers to align the written, the supported, and the assessed curricula. Because these three types are closely related, the alignment can be accomplished in one project. The following process has worked well with several school systems.

1. *Plan the project.* Appoint a curriculum alignment committee (or use an existing committee) to oversee and coordinate the project. Train the committee in the alignment process as it involves these three types of curriculum. The alignment committee should then train the grade-level teams, who will carry out the alignment tasks for their grade.

2. *Focus the curriculum.* The grade-level teams should carefully analyze the new district curriculum to focus the alignment process on the mastery objectives. As the term is used here, the mastery objectives are those that meet one or more of the following criteria:

- Will likely be tested or assessed
- Require explicit teaching
- Are best learned when they are carefully planned
- Are essential for all students to master

These mastery objectives are different from what we have termed *continuing development objectives,* those outcomes that should be nurtured on every suitable occasion, not taught in a specific grade level. Here is an example to show the difference:

- *Mastery:* Define metaphor.
- *Continuing development:* Enjoy poetry.

Mastery objectives should be aligned with tests and texts; organic outcomes need not be.

The complete set of mastery objectives should be stored in a computerized database, organized by grade level and then by areas within that subject. Various curriculum alignment and mapping programs are available for this purpose.

3. *Check to be sure that the district curriculum embodies the state standards.* The state standards will surely be reflected in state tests; they also provide useful guidelines for local developers.

4. *Analyze the tests.* Using a printout of the mastery objectives for their grade level, the teams should then indicate on an appropriate form which of the mastery objectives are likely to be tested. An example of the form that can be used in this process is shown in Table 10.1. In determining which mastery objectives are likely to be tested, the team should analyze state tests, district tests, and standardized tests. They need not analyze teacher-made tests because the assumption is that teachers will test what they have taught. In analyzing those tests, the team can use descriptions of test content and previously given tests that are no longer considered confidential.

TABLE 10.1

Curriculum Alignment Form

Subject: English language arts		Grade: 9
Mastery Objectives	Tested	Text: English 9
Define, identify metaphor	x	pp. 123–126
Listen critically		
Write personal narrative	x	pp. 16–17
Hold interview		p. 14

5. *Analyze the texts.* The final step is to determine where the mastery objectives are explained in the text. The team should check the table of contents and the index of the texts used, noting the page numbers where the topic is treated. The team should enter page numbers only if the topic is treated in sufficient depth. Textbooks often treat topics so superficially that the text can be of little value to teachers and students.

6. *Evaluate the results.* The alignment committee should review all the work of the teams, noting any problems that need correcting and producing a complete set for the entire school. This complete set will be useful for the principal and supervisors.

7. *Use the results.* Simply completing the alignment charts has little value. The results should be used to accomplish two tasks. First, as noted briefly below and explained more fully in Chapters 12 and 13, teachers should use the list of mastery objectives to develop yearly and unit plans that ensure adequate treatment of all these objectives. Mastery objectives that are tested should receive the highest priority in planning for learning; continuing development objectives likely to be tested would have a second priority. Second, the team should institute plans to fill in any gaps in the textbook. They can order supplementary materials or write their own materials.

ALIGNING THE WRITTEN
AND THE TAUGHT CURRICULA

The alignment charts described above can be very useful in aligning the written and the taught curricula. Next to aligning the taught and the learned curricula, this is probably the most important alignment of all. Even the most conscientious teachers will need help to ensure that they are effectively delivering the written curriculum. As explained more fully in Chapters 12 and 13, the principal should help teachers develop yearly calendars and unit plans. In developing such plans, the teacher should systematically check off the mastery objectives as they are scheduled in the yearly calendar and included in the unit. When the principal reviews these plans, he or she should check to ensure that all mastery objectives are in fact included.

ALIGNING THE HIDDEN
AND THE LEARNED CURRICULA

Because the hidden curriculum has such an impact on student learning, it deserves special study by the principal and teachers. The principal may therefore wish to lead a special task force to make a systematic analysis. Here are the main factors that seem to constitute the hidden curriculum:

- *Time allocation:* For example, are health and physical education allocated sufficient time to change the behavior of children and youth?
- *Space allocation:* How much space is allocated for teacher conferring and planning?
- *Use of discretionary funds:* How are such funds expended, and who decides this?
- *Student discipline:* Do suspensions seem to reflect an ethnic bias?
- *Physical appearance:* Does the appearance of facilities suggest that those in the building care for the school? Are walls decorated with student artwork?
- *Student activities program:* Does this program reflect and respond to student talent diversity?

- *Communication:* Are most of the messages over the public address system of a positive nature? How often are student voices heard?
- *Power:* Do teachers have power in the decision-making process? Do students have any real power over the factors that matter?

When the analysis of the hidden curriculum has been completed, the principal and the teachers should identify those hidden messages that do not reflect what they want students to learn—then work together to alter discrepant elements. For example, if the principal and teachers believe in the importance of students' artistic creativity but discover that the hidden curriculum contains no traces of creativity, they might want to change the hidden curriculum by decorating the corridors with student artwork.

ALIGNING THE TAUGHT AND THE LEARNED CURRICULA

The final and perhaps most important type of alignment involves the taught and the learned curricula. Whereas teachers mistakenly assume that students learn all that they are taught, the evidence is otherwise. As Doyle (1986) points out in his review of the research, for much of classroom time, students are either obviously off-task or merely feigning on-task behavior, only dimly aware of what the teacher is trying to teach.

This issue is so important that the principal and the teachers should discuss it in a faculty meeting or special workshop that would answer four questions: What is the taught/learned gap, and why is it important? What student factors cause it? What can teachers do to reduce the gap? What next steps should we take?

Nature and Importance of the Gap

The session should begin with an open dialogue about the gap at the school. A simple definition should be helpful: "Students do not learn all that teachers teach. We call that the . . . taught/learned . . . gap." A brief discussion of its importance can follow.

Student Factors

The next part of the discussion is to examine the student factors that cause the taught/learned gap. Both the research and our experience indicate that the following elements are crucial.

First, students have limited attention spans. They have other agendas. The teacher may be doing his or her best to teach the parts of the amoeba, but student minds are on weekend activities. All that television watching has conditioned them to expect one-minute messages. Also, the physical environment may cause inattention. If the room is too warm, for example, students will find it difficult to focus on a complex task.

Students may also lack knowledge and cognitive development. They are doing the best they can, but what they are hearing does not make sense. The terms are too difficult; the new knowledge is overwhelming. Students also may have special needs that are not being addressed. Even though they may not have obvious disabilities, they may have learning problems that interfere with their learning.

Peer pressure may also interfere with the learning process. This factor often has an especially negative impact on economically disadvantaged minority students. They may want to learn, but a few powerful peers can establish norms that devalue learning.

Teacher-Facilitating Factors

In an atmosphere of inquiry, with teachers discussing their experience, the faculty should next analyze what seems to work. This discussion should have a positive tone so that teachers do not feel they are being blamed. The following teaching strategies will probably be identified:

1. Clarify the objective.

2. Help students find meaning and purpose in learning the objective.

3. Encourage students to ask questions.

4. Use learning strategies that require a high level of student activity.

5. Use frequent quizzing to monitor learning and maintain high alertness.

6. Observe for verbal and nonverbal signs of off-task behavior.

7. Use monitoring data to adjust instruction.

The workshop should end with a discussion of what can be done to determine how much of a gap exists and what can be done to reduce it. The following process should be useful:

1. Teachers pair off or work in collegial teams.

2. Teacher A plans a lesson with the help of Teacher B; they also prepare a comprehensive quiz based on that lesson.

3. Teacher A implements the lesson, while Teacher B observes both student and teacher behavior.

4. Teacher A administers the quiz at the end of the lesson.

5. They meet to discuss the results.

6. They then switch roles.

CHAPTER SUMMARY

This chapter examines the types of curricula and the types of alignment needed among the different curriculum types. Suggestions are offered on how to approach the alignment process, how to identify curriculum gaps, and how student factors and teacher factors must be considered in the gap analysis. Curriculum alignment is a high-value activity for schools, and even if external consultants are used to assist, principal ownership and leadership are essential. The next chapter focuses on monitoring the implementation of the curriculum.

REFERENCES

Brown, D. S. (1988). Twelve middle-school teachers' planning. *Elementary School Journal, 89,* 69–87.

Doyle, W. (1986). Classroom organization and management. In M. C. Wittrock (Ed.), *Handbook of research on teaching* (3rd ed., pp. 392–431). New York: Macmillan.

English, F. W. (2000). *Deciding what to teach and test: Developing, aligning, and auditing the curriculum* (millennium ed.). Thousand Oaks, CA: Corwin Press.

English, F. W., & Steffy, B. E. (2001). *Deep curriculum alignment: Creating a level playing field for all children on high-stakes tests of educational accountability.* Lanham, MD: Scarecrow.

Kendall, J. S., & Marzano, R. J. (2007). *Content knowledge: A compendium of standards and benchmarks for K–12 education* (4th ed.). Aurora, CO: Midcontinent Regional Educational Laboratory. Retrieved October 22, 2007, from www.mcrel.org/standards-benchmarks/

National Council of Teachers of English and International Reading Association. (1996). *Standards for the English language arts.* Urbana, IL: National Council of Teachers of English. Retrieved October 21, 2007, from www.ncte.org/store/books/standards/105977.htm

National Council of Teachers of Mathematics. (2000). *Principles and standards for school mathematics.* Reston, VA: Author. Retrieved March 21, 2008, from www.nctm.org/standards/default.aspx?id=58

Wikimedia Foundation. (2007). *Change issues in curriculum and instruction/ curriculum, textbook, and pedagogy.* From Wikibooks, the open-content textbooks collection. Retrieved October 21, 2007, from the Wikibooks open-content textbooks collection Web site: http://en.wiki books.org

CHAPTER ELEVEN

Monitoring the Implementation Process

I t has often been said that "what gets monitored, gets done." The monitoring of the curriculum involves the use of processes to determine to what extent the approved curriculum has been implemented. This chapter reviews the argument about monitoring and presents a model that maintains the advantages of monitoring while avoiding its drawbacks. The model can be used both as a basis for monitoring and as a guide for helping teachers implement the whole curriculum, not just emphasizing the tested curriculum.

THE ARGUMENT ABOUT MONITORING

Monitoring the implementation of curriculum is one of those issues that seem to be highly controversial and divisive. On the one hand, many policymakers and administrators seem to distrust teachers, spending much time developing and implementing elaborate teacher-accountability systems. On the other hand, some experts in the field seem to believe that there should be no monitoring, with each teacher developing his or her own curriculum. Therefore, a review of the reasons advanced by each camp seems in order.

Reasons for Monitoring

Why should principals monitor the curriculum? Several reasons have been advanced. The first is simply efficiency: the district has spent a great deal of time and money on developing the curriculum, and it would be a manifest waste if teachers simply ignored it. The second is consistent development: if the district curriculum has been carefully sequenced and articulated, monitoring will help ensure that what students are taught in fourth grade builds on third and leads into fifth. Also, monitoring keeps the teachers alert and on task. If they know that their choice of curriculum content is being monitored, they will more likely select appropriate content from the guide. Finally, from the principal's perspective, monitoring is a useful process for helping the principal become more visible and involved with curriculum, one of the central components of school improvement.

There is some research support for these claims (see Cotton, 1995). Without monitoring and left to their own devices, teachers tend to emphasize what they know best, without being overly concerned with the district curriculum. For example, elementary teachers tend to slight science and emphasize reading, if they are not monitored. Also, the research is clear that a carefully articulated curriculum leads to improved achievement, especially in mathematics in which grade-to-grade coordination is so crucial (Newmann, Smith, Allensworth, & Bryk, 2001).

Reasons for Not Monitoring

Those who oppose monitoring also advance several persuasive reasons. First, they are concerned that very close monitoring implies distrust of teachers and, therefore, damages the school climate by placing administrators and teachers in adversarial roles. Second, insisting that the standard curriculum be faithfully implemented for all students ignores the reality of student and school differences. Many of those monitoring systems currently take the form of complex instructional management and accountability systems. Also, close monitoring with a concomitant emphasis on test scores forces the teacher to focus on testlike items, thus narrowing the curriculum and overemphasizing direct instruction. Finally, excessive monitoring reduces the teacher to a mechanical implementer of what others have produced, thus deskilling teaching.

Here again, there is some evidence to support these claims. Miller's (1996) study of the Kentucky state accountability system (which emphasized close monitoring and teacher accountability for test results) concluded that it had no measurable impact on student achievement; it instead drove a wedge between teachers, parents, and schools and undermined teachers' sense of efficacy. Also, McNeil's (2000) and Bushnell's (2003) study confirmed some of the worst fears of opponents of monitoring: The emphasis on monitoring and test scores resulted in a classroom characterized by a focus on testable learning, drill and practice on testlike items, and excessive use of direct instruction.

However, NCLB and its range of sanctions for schools not making Adequate Yearly Progress (AYP) has led to more accountability, more monitoring, and more testing. In some cases, schools and systems have performed better with additional accountability. We contend that strong curriculum leadership by the principal that leads to effective teaching and learning will lead to improved achievement outcomes without undue preoccupation with testing.

A PRACTICAL SOLUTION

Over several years of working with school districts and reviewing the research, we have developed a monitoring system that maintains the advantages while avoiding the drawbacks of monitoring. Also, using handheld digital devices during classroom walk-throughs can facilitate the monitoring process.

Establishing the Antecedent Conditions

Monitoring efforts are more likely to succeed if certain antecedent conditions are present.

- *Emphasize mutual accomplishment, not total fidelity.* Mutual accomplishment (first identified by Bird, 1986) is a type of implementation in which the developers of an innovation (the district curriculum workers) accomplish their central goal of changing the curriculum and the users of the innovation (classroom teachers) accomplish their goals of influencing the curriculum and maintaining control of the essential elements of classroom life. Mutual accomplishment is a win/win philosophy of curriculum implementation. Working for complete fidelity is a win/lose approach: administrators win and teachers lose.

- *Influence the development of a "teacher friendly" and "change-simple" curriculum.* As explained throughout this work, a teacher-friendly curriculum is one with these features: (a) it specifically provides time and space for teacher enrichment, (b) it is presented in a form that makes it easily accessible, and (c) it does not mandate a sequence or teaching approach. A change-simple curriculum is one that reflects the characteristics that Fullan (2001) has found are important in bringing about effective change. First, the curriculum is clear: terms are defined clearly, and objectives are specified unambiguously. Second, the curriculum avoids excessive complexity: it does not expect the teacher to use too many resources, use complicated technology, or keep too many elements in mind. Finally, the curriculum is one of high quality: teachers respect it and wish to implement it.
- *Establish a culture that values continuous improvement and collaboration.* This is perhaps the most crucial antecedent condition. The principal should take leadership in clarifying the concept of continuous improvement, of emphasizing its role in making the school better, in modeling that philosophy, and in rewarding teachers who manifest it. Teachers should understand that curriculum development is an ongoing, embedded process, not a single event.

Systematic collaboration is the other critical element in the school's culture. The principal should establish the importance of working together in a cooperative manner; establish conditions that support collaboration, such as organized professional learning community structures; model collaboration; and reward teachers who cooperate. As Reeves (2006) has pointed out, such an attitude is especially crucial in developing a supportive environment for curriculum change.

Taking Effective Action to Achieve Mutual Accomplishment

Once those antecedent conditions have been established, principals can then take effective action to achieve mutual accomplishment.

- *Ensure that resources are available in a timely manner.* Principals can help by putting pressure on district personnel to order new texts and other materials early enough to ensure that they are on hand for teachers' use. Teachers often express great frustration when essential materials do not arrive on time.

- *Provide ongoing staff development that is sensitive to teachers' stages of concern.* Though the district is primarily responsible for providing the basic staff development required by the new curriculum, the principal should also take the initiative in ensuring that teachers have time to meet together to exchange ideas, share strategies, and solve common problems. Here, the research on teachers' stages of concern should be useful (see Hall, Hord, George, Stiegelbauer, & Dirksen, 2006). In the early stages of developing a curriculum, teachers simply want to be kept informed. Their concerns later shift to personal issues: How will the new curriculum affect me? Only in later stages will they typically ask questions about its impact on student learning.

- *Help teachers translate the district guide into long-term plans.* As explained more fully in Chapters 12 and 13, yearly planning calendars and units of study enable the teachers to translate the district guide into planning documents that teachers can use as they plan for instruction. The district guide by itself is not sufficient as a guide to such planning; this additional work is necessary. Once teachers have developed long-term and unit plans, the principal can confer with them in a climate of dialogue. These questions can be raised:
  - Have all the mastery objectives been suitably emphasized?
  - Do time allocations reflect curricular and assessment priorities?
  - Will the sequence likely lead to mastery?

- *Make several informal observations.* As explained more fully in Glatthorn, Boschee, and Whitehead (2006), informal observations are short drop-in visits to classrooms, lasting only five to ten minutes. In this brief period, the principal can observe to what extent the district curriculum is being implemented or enriched. If three such informal observations indicate that the teacher is spending too much time on unrelated curriculum issues, the principal can inquire in a constructive manner about the teacher's rationale for seeming to deviate from the curriculum.

The informal observations should not be used to evaluate teachers. Rather, they are an effective monitoring strategy. They also serve as a means of giving the teacher merited and timely praise—or as a distant early warning system of problems that may need systematic attention.

- *Cheer for the curriculum.* The principal can serve as a cheerleader for the new curriculum and remind teachers of the need for effective implementation.
- *Analyze assessments and test scores with teachers.* Although teachers should not be held totally accountable for students' test results, they should cooperate with the principal in examining schoolwide and classroom-specific results with an analytical perspective. Such a perspective examines systematically the following issues related to the alignment of curriculum, instruction, and assessment:
    - o Were the test and any other types of assessments congruent with the goals, benchmarks, and content of the curriculum?
    - o Were the texts and other instructional materials congruent with the curriculum?
    - o Was sufficient time devoted to the content included in the test?
    - o Were students motivated to master the curriculum and perform well on the test?
    - o Did parents provide a supportive learning environment at home and emphasize the importance of the tests?
    - o Did teachers use effective instructional approaches?
    - o Was the curriculum itself of high quality?
    - o Which groups of students performed below expectations? Do they need additional time, more varied materials, or diversified teaching/learning activities?

    This analysis should be carried out in an atmosphere of problem solving and a quest for continuous improvement, not blaming or scapegoating.

CHAPTER SUMMARY

This chapter examines arguments for and against monitoring of the curriculum. It suggests how such a system may operate and recommends that mutual accomplishment is a win/win philosophy of curriculum implementation. Any monitoring system that balances the need for district curriculum coordination with the teachers' need for a measure of autonomy can be effective if it is implemented in a climate that supports continuous improvement and collegiality. The system described above has worked effectively for many school systems and schools, but principals and teachers are strongly encouraged to develop their own model in a culture of collaboration. Part IV explores many ways in which leaders can work with teachers on curriculum issues.

REFERENCES

Bird, T. (1986). Mutual adaptation and mutual accomplishment: Images of change in a field experiment. In A. Lieberman (Ed.), *Re-thinking school improvement: Research, craft, and concept* (pp. 45–60). Alexandria, VA: Association for Supervision and Curriculum Development.

Bushnell, M. (2003). Teachers in the schoolhouse panopticon: Complicity and resistance. *Education and Urban Society, 35*(3), 251–272. The online version of this article can be found at http://eus.sagepub.com/cgi/content/abstract/35/3/251

Cotton, K. (1995). *Effective schooling practices: A research synthesis, 1995 update.* Portland, OR: Northwest Regional Educational Laboratory.

Fullan, M. G. (2001). *The new meaning of educational change* (3rd ed.). New York: Teachers College.

Glatthorn, A. A., Boschee, F., & Whitehead, B. M. (2006). *Curriculum leadership: Development and implementation.* Thousand Oaks, CA: Sage.

Hall, G. E., Hord, S. M., George, A. A., Stiegelbauer, S., & Dirksen, D. (2006). *Measuring implementation in schools: The concerns based adoption model.* Austin, TX: Southwest Educational Development Laboratory.

McNeil, L. M. (2000). *Contradictions of school reform: Educational costs of standardized testing.* New York: Routledge.

Miller, E. (1996, January/February). Early reports from Kentucky on cash rewards for "successful" schools reveal many problems. *Harvard Education Letter, 12,* 1–3.

Newmann, F. M., Smith, B. A., Allensworth, E., & Bryk, A. S. (2001). Instructional program coherence: What it is and why it should guide school improvement policy. *Educational Evaluation and Policy Analysis, 23*(4), 297–321.

Reeves, D. B. (2006). *The learning leader: How to focus school improvement for better results.* Alexandria, VA: Association for Supervision and Curriculum Development.

PART IV

Working With Teachers

CHAPTER TWELVE

Making Yearly Planning Calendars

The district curriculum guide is only a foundation for teachers' planning. Effective principals know how to help teachers use the guide to develop yearly and unit plans. This chapter explains the nature of yearly plans, provides a rationale for their use, suggests one way of organizing for yearly planning, and presents a process by which a faculty can collaborate in the development and review of such plans. Chapter 13 then explains how teachers can use the yearly plan as a basis for unit planning. (Those interested in a full discussion of how teachers plan should consult Clark & Peterson, 1986; Cooper & Kiger, 2007; Schmidt, Porter, Floden, Freeman, & Schwille, 1987; Weiss, Pasley, Smith, Banilower, & Heck, 2003.)

THE NATURE OF YEARLY PLANS AND A RATIONALE FOR THEIR USE

Yearly plans are documents, usually in calendar form, that show the units that the teacher will teach through the course of the year. They may also indicate significant events occurring in the school community that will affect teaching and learning and identify the mastery benchmarks to be emphasized. In those schools in which subjects are taught intensively for one term rather than for an entire year, the term plan is substituted for the yearly plan.

For several reasons, the yearly plan is a very useful document. It is recommended that teachers work together in producing the plan, thereby fostering collaborative planning by a grade-level or subject team. The yearly plan provides a foundation for the more detailed unit plans by translating the curriculum guide into a series of units. It facilitates coordination across subject lines; as explained more fully later, it provides a simple means of examining the flow of instruction in two or more related subjects. It operationalizes the school's decisions with respect to curriculum integration. It shows the sequence of units across the year. And it shows clearly the time allocations teachers have made for the several units, thus providing a useful tool for curriculum monitoring.

Though the yearly plan has several reasons for recommending it, not all teachers are enthusiastic about developing and using yearly plans. Some see them as simply one more administrative requirement. Others complain that school life is so unpredictable that no plan can be an accurate portrayal of the actual teaching and learning that go on in the classroom. Given such teacher opposition, the principal needs to lay the groundwork, as explained below.

ORGANIZING FOR YEARLY PLANNING

Each school will use its own system for accomplishing the planning process. The procedures explained below have worked well with several schools.

Develop the Proposal

The first phase is to develop the school's proposal for yearly planning. The principal should introduce the concept of yearly planning during the spring semester, so that decisions can be made in a timely manner for the following school year. In a faculty meeting devoted just to this topic, the principal (or one of the teacher-leaders) should make a 15-minute presentation on the concept of, and rationale for, yearly planning. Following that presentation, the teachers should meet in small groups to discuss their views and their present practice with respect to yearly planning, reporting the results of the group discussions to the entire faculty. If there seems to be general support for the process, the principal can then move into the next phase.

If there is strong opposition, then further study is indicated. In this instance, the principal should take the time to explore more deeply the reasons for opposition and work with teachers to remove the obstacles that cause them to question the value of planning.

Once sufficient support has been developed, the principal should ask a special task force (or one of the existing school committees) to develop a specific proposal for faculty to examine. By reviewing this chapter, analyzing the literature, visiting schools using such plans, and sharing their own experience and knowledge, the task force should make a series of recommendations about the following issues (our own recommendations are explained more fully in the following sections):

- The format for yearly planning
- The contents of the yearly plans
- The structure by which plans will be produced—team, department, or individual
- The review process
- The schedule for developing yearly plans

For each issue, a specific recommendation is made in the next section; however, it is important for the faculty to decide these matters. Once the proposal has been reviewed and revised, it should be adopted and disseminated as the school's process for yearly planning.

Though schools will vary in how they accomplish this initial organizing task, the principal should ensure that the school's planning structure and processes have been developed with significant teacher input.

Lay the Foundations

The next phase in the process is to establish the foundations for yearly planning.

1. *Develop the forms.* This is a crucial step, because the forms will also dictate content. Table 12.1 shows one form that has been used successfully with many schools; Table 12.2 shows a form that elementary teachers seem to prefer. The form in Table 12.1 includes four essential planning items:

    a. The weeks of the school year, in sequence
    b. For each week, any events that will affect teaching and learning, including the following: national and state holidays, parent meetings, student extracurricular activities,

teacher work days, and report card and parent conference days.

c. The title of the unit

d. The related mastery benchmarks

Some schools find it useful to add a column for the textbook pages that support the unit.

The alternative form shows the four main subjects taught by elementary teachers in one column and the units indicated for each week. Though it lacks some of the details of the standard form, its chief advantage is that it shows how the several subjects relate to each other.

2. *Provide the training.* One 2-hour training session for the entire faculty should be sufficient to introduce the form and do practice exercises to review the skills needed to complete it. Follow-up sessions can be held at the team level. The next section of this chapter can provide the knowledge base for staff development.

3. *Establish deadlines for submission of plans.* Some principals with whom we have worked report that the following approach is highly effective. Recommend to teachers that,

TABLE 12.1

Recommended Form for Yearly Planning

Team: English II		Date submitted: 9/23	
Weeks of Year	*Important Events*	*Unit Title*	*Mastery Benchmarks*
1/13–17	M. L. King, Jr.'s birthday	Transformational leaders	Write persuasive letter
1/20–24		Transformational leaders	Write contrast/ compare letter

TABLE 12.2

Alternative Form: Elementary

Team: Fifth grade	Date submitted: 9/23		
	Weeks & Topics		
Subjects	*1/13–17*	*1/20–24*	*1/27–31*
Language arts	Opinion letter		
Social studies	Great leaders		
Science	Life in winter		
Math	Factoring		

in the summer, they develop standard plans for the first four weeks of school. They will use those four weeks to assess student readiness, determine student needs, go over class routines, and introduce the subject. Then, with this knowledge of the students and the curriculum in mind, they will develop a sound plan for the rest of the year.

4. *Provide blocks of planning time for teams to collaborate on the planning.* With the above preparations complete, one half-day work session should be sufficient to accomplish the planning process.

DEVELOPING YEARLY PLANS

There are several processes that teams can use in developing the yearly plan. Several teams have found the following one to be effective and efficient. (The process assumes that the team is using the form shown in Table 12.1 to plan one subject.)

1. *Complete the basic information.* The team should note the team's name, list the weeks of the school year, and include the important events.

2. *Identify the titles of the units to be taught.* The unit title should indicate the main focus of the unit. Four steps are involved here:

a. The team should analyze the curriculum guide carefully, listing the mastery benchmarks in the order in which they are presented in the guide. The team should asterisk the objectives likely to be tested in state and district tests.

b. The team should determine the organizing principle to be used in grouping the mastery benchmarks. The objectives have probably been listed in the guide according to some logical categorization of general goals. The teachers may use this goal-based classification system or one of these alternatives: complex skills ("Writing the Personal Narrative"), time periods ("The Industrial Age"), themes ("Families First"), problems ("Cleaning Up the Environment"), major works of art ("The Book of Job"), or literary or artistic genres ("The Nature of Tragedy").

c. The team should next check the texts to be used. Teachers who have a somewhat shallow knowledge of the subject may find the textbook organization the simplest way to identify unit titles.

d. The team should make a tentative list of unit titles and then refine it through discussion and assessment. The titles should then be noted on the form.

3. *Determine the sequence of units.* Once the tentative list of titles has been developed, the team should decide on the order of units. Several sequencing principles are available. Units can be organized according to students' interests, beginning with a unit that has high interest and using seasonal progression to determine placement of other units. Alternatively, they can be organized according to content difficulty, starting with units that are relatively simple and moving to more challenging ones. They can also be ordered chronologically, as they often are in history courses or courses emphasizing British or American literature. Another method of sequencing is the "expanding horizons" approach, beginning with the individual, then the family, then the community, followed by the state and the nation. Finally, units can be organized in relation to the

structure of that subject, as mathematics units usually are. A team could also combine two or more of these principles.

4. *Allocate time to each unit.* The time can perhaps best be represented by the number of instructional periods to be devoted to the unit; an instructional period is defined as a clearly demarcated session lasting from 30 to 50 minutes. This is how the team should proceed:

    a. Calculate the total number of instructional periods available.
    b. Determine the relative importance of each unit according to district and school priorities.
    c. Consider the attention span of the students.
    d. Assess the complexity of the unit, keeping in mind the importance of students achieving depth of understanding.
    e. Tentatively allocate periods to each unit.
    f. Translate the periods to lessons and to weeks.

5. *Record information on a yearly calendar.* All of the above information should be recorded on a yearly calendar.

6. *Relate curriculum guide mastery benchmarks to units.* Do one final check to be sure that all the mastery skills and knowledge have been included in the units. Perhaps the easiest way to do this is to note in the curriculum guide in which unit each mastery benchmark is emphasized.

REVIEWING THE PLANS

Once the grade-level or subject team has produced and evaluated their calendar, the principal should review it. The first step is to review the calendars individually, using the criteria listed in Table 12.3.

Once all the individual calendars have been reviewed, the principal should examine the calendars for a given grade level to see if appropriate correlation exists between related subjects, such as science and mathematics or English language arts and social studies. Then the principal should examine the calendars for a given subject to assess the grade-to-grade progression, ensuring that there is no undue repetition.

TABLE 12.3

Criteria for Evaluating Yearly Calendars

Does the yearly planning calendar . . .

- Reflect and correspond with the school calendar?
- Note significant events likely to influence teaching and learning?
- Organize the objectives into units with titles clearly stated?
- Sequence the units appropriately?
- Allocate time appropriately?
- Ensure that all mastery benchmarks are included?
- Reflect the importance of students achieving depth of understanding?

CHAPTER SUMMARY

This chapter explains the nature and usefulness of yearly plans, suggests one way of organizing the yearly planning process, and shows how the principal and faculty can collaborate in the development and review of such plans. The importance of this planning activity is that it communicates the big picture for curriculum and develops stakeholder ownership and commitment. From yearly plans, we move to unit development in the next chapter.

REFERENCES

Clark, C. M., & Peterson, P. L. (1986). Teachers' thought processes. In M. C. Wittrock (Ed.), *Handbook of research on teaching* (3rd ed., pp. 255–296). New York: McMillan.

Cooper, J. D., & Kiger, N. D. (2007). *Literacy assessment—Helping teachers plan instruction* (3rd ed.). New York: Houghton Mifflin.

Schmidt, W. H., Porter, A. C., Floden, R. E., Freeman, D. J., & Schwille, J. R. (1987). Four patterns of teacher content decision making. *Journal of Curriculum Studies, 19,* 439–455.

Weiss, I. R., Pasley, J. D., Smith, P. S., Banilower, E. R., & Heck, D. J. (2003). *Looking inside the classroom: A study of K–12 mathematics and science education in the United States.* Chapel Hill, NC: Horizon Research. Retrieved October 22, 2007, from www.horizon-research .com/insidetheclassroom/reports/looking/complete.pdf

CHAPTER THIRTEEN

Developing Units of Study

W ith the yearly planning calendar developed, teachers are ready to move to the next level of planning—the unit. This chapter begins with a rationale for unit development, suggests a systematic way to organize teachers to implement effective unit development, and explains in detail a process for developing units based on constructivist principles.

A RATIONALE FOR UNIT DEVELOPMENT

Many teachers never move beyond short-term planning: they plan for one week or one day at a time. As a result, their teaching often seems fragmented and disjointed. Many principals reinforce this emphasis on short-term planning by checking daily lesson plans, ignoring the need to help teachers develop units.

Instead, principals should help teachers develop units, because unit planning has several advantages. First, unit planning stresses the holistic nature of learning: students see the big picture rather than bits and pieces that do not seem to fit together. Second, the unit is the best level at which to integrate the curriculum. Whereas individual lessons can be integrated, the unit structure, in its emphasis on general concepts and themes, is a more effective vehicle for integration. Units also provide the best means for emphasizing skills across the curriculum—reading, writing, and studying. These skills—useful in most subjects—are easier to build into a unit structure than teach as stand-alone lessons. Also, the unit is the optimal level for enabling students to develop and apply problem-solving skills. Solving complex problems by drawing on a deep knowledge base takes time. Finally, the unit lends itself to the use of authentic assessment measures. Most units should culminate in the demonstration of learning.

Some teachers will resist an emphasis on unit planning. The reasons are understandable. Unit planning is more difficult than daily lesson planning and requires skills that many teachers lack. Unit planning takes more time, a precious commodity for teachers. And in too many instances, unit planning seems to be a hit-or-miss process that teachers do in isolation, without help or encouragement. Principals need to exercise active leadership in helping teachers understand the importance of unit planning and accomplish the task in a more systematic manner.

ORGANIZING FOR UNIT DEVELOPMENT

To avoid hit-or-miss planning, principals should develop the structures and plans needed for long-term systematic development. One suggested process is explained below.

Lay the Foundations

Begin by establishing a central planning group or assigning the central planning responsibilities to an existing committee or council. That group should complete the following steps:

1. *Identify the resources needed and develop a proposal to secure them.* Long-term unit planning requires resources— time, funds, materials, and expertise. Although funds are always limited, the planning group should work with the principal to develop a proposal for getting special funding from a variety of sources: the school board, federal and state programs, grants, foundations, and parent organizations.

2. *Organize unit development teams.* At the outset at least, all teachers should be involved in a team approach to unit development. Later on, if teachers prefer to work independently, they may do so. In the initial stage, however, they will profit

more from interaction and collaboration with colleagues. In elementary and middle schools, the teams will probably be organized by grade level; in high school, by subject.

3. *Decide how quality time can best be provided.* Teachers are not likely to produce quality units if they are required to do so after a long day of teaching. Instead, they need quality time. How this can be provided without unduly reducing instructional time is a complicated matter for the planners to consider; they may examine alternatives such as summer workshops, early dismissals, inservice days, and common planning periods.

4. *Provide the initial training needed to help teams get started.* Staff development to support unit planning should be an ongoing process rather than a one-shot, random intervention. The initial phase should concentrate on the skills teachers need to begin their work effectively.

Make the Basic Decisions

The planning group should next make the basic decisions needed to get the project off the ground, securing teacher input in resolving the following issues:

- *What standard format should we use?* Although the specifics of format will vary from school to school, all units should include the following basic information: name and address of school district, name and address of school, title of unit, names of developers, date of publication, grade level, and subject.
- *What content criteria should we use?* One good way to promote quality is to establish and reinforce specific content criteria. Table 13.1 provides a suggested list.
- *Shall we begin with mastery or enrichment units?* The recommendation here is to begin with mastery units, adding enrichment if there is sufficient time and interest.
- *Shall we begin with subject-focused or integrated units?* The answer will depend, of course, on the school's decision about integration, as explained in Chapter 9. In general, it is better to begin with subject-focused units because they are easier to develop. Integrated units are a next step.

TABLE 13.1

Curriculum Content Criteria

All units developed for Morris Middle School students will include the following:

- A clear statement of the unit goal or the general outcome to be achieved
- Time allocation for teaching the unit
- Benchmarks and specific learning objectives derived from the goal
- Learning activities that will enable students to achieve the objectives
- Suggestions for remediating learning
- Resources for the unit
- Methods for assessing student learning, including preassessments for learning

- *What review process shall we employ?* All units should first be reviewed by the team of developers. Then they should be submitted to the central planning group for further evaluation.
- *What storage-and-retrieval system shall we use?* If the school has the know-how and the software needed, units can be stored in the computer, in a commercial curriculum management system, in shared online folders, or on flash drives. Otherwise, develop a central library accessible to teachers.
- *What schedule can be implemented for accomplishing the project?* A realistic schedule, showing for each grade or subject the units to be developed and the deadlines for developing them, will help keep the project moving.

DEVELOPING UNITS BASED ON CONSTRUCTIVIST PRINCIPLES

There are many models of unit development that teams can use in their planning. However, principals and teachers are strongly encouraged to use a constructivist model, as it is strongly supported by current research in cognitive psychology. Constructivism emphasizes the learner as an active maker or constructor of meaning and places contextualized problem solving at the center of all learning. The following discussion reviews the basic principles of constructivism and then presents in greater detail a process for developing units based on a constructivist perspective.

The Basic Principles of Constructivism

Although each expert conceptualizes constructivism from a slightly different perspective, certain general principles can be synthesized from the literature. (The discussion below draws from Brooks & Brooks, 1999; Gray, 1997; Cornelius-White, 2007; Marzano, Pickering, Arredondo, & Paynter, 1997; and McCombs, 2003.)

The Nature of Learning

In considering the nature of learning, constructivism posits nine basic tenets:

1. *Learning is not a passive, receptive process but is instead an active, meaning-making process.* It is the ability to perform complex cognitive tasks that require the active use and application of knowledge in solving meaningful problems.

2. *Thus, learning at its best involves conceptual change—modifying one's previous understanding of concepts so that they are more complex and more valid.* Typically, the learner begins with a naive or inaccurate concept; the learning process enables the learner to develop a deeper or truer understanding of the concept.

3. *In this sense, learning is always subjective and personal.* The learner best learns when he or she can internalize what is being learned, representing it through learner-generated symbols, metaphors, images, graphics, and models.

4. *Learning is also situated or contextualized.* Students should carry out tasks and solve problems that resemble the nature of those tasks in the real world. Rather than doing "exercises" out of context, the students learn to solve contextualized problems.

5. *Learning is social.* Learning at its best develops from inter-action with others as perceptions are shared, information is exchanged, and problems are solved collaboratively.

6. *Learning is affective.* Cognition and affect are closely related. The extent and nature of learning are influenced by the fol-lowing affective elements: self-awareness and beliefs about one's abilities, clarity and strength of learning goals, personal expectations, general state of mind, and motivation to learn.

7. *The nature of the learning task is crucial.* The best learning tasks are characterized by these features: optimal difficulty in relation to the learner's development, relevancy to the learner's needs, authenticity with respect to the real world, and challenge and novelty for the learner.

8. *Learning is strongly influenced by the learner's development.* Learners move through identifiable stages of physical, intel-lectual, emotional, and social growth that affect what can be learned and in what depth of understanding. Learners seem to do best when the learning is at their proximal stage of devel-opment, challenging enough to require them to stretch but attainable with effort.

9. *Learning at its best involves metacognition.* The student reflects about his or her learning throughout the entire learn-ing process.

The Role of the Teacher

Constructivism also requires a change in the teacher's role. In the constructivist approach, the teacher carries out six essential functions, as Educational Broadcasting Corporation (2004), DeVries, (2002), and Gray (1997) note.

1. *Modeling:* The teacher performs the task so that the students can observe and build a conceptual model of the processes.

2. *Coaching:* The teacher observes the students as they carry out a task and offers hints, feedback, and modeling.

3. *Scaffolding and fading:* The term *scaffolding* is a metaphor for cognitive structure. At the initial stages of the learning process, the learner seems to function best with a good deal

of structure, using teacher-provided cues, specific explanations, and organizing strategies to make sense of the problem and to engage in its solution. As the learner progresses, he or she needs less scaffolding; the goal is to fade gradually to turn over the entire process to the learner so that he or she becomes self-regulating.

4. *Articulation:* The teacher helps the students articulate their knowledge and their reasoning processes to make the cognitive processes visible.

5. *Reflection:* The teacher helps the students reflect about their processes and compare them with those of an expert or another student.

6. *Exploration:* The teacher pushes students to do problem solving on their own—to frame questions and to find answers.

The Importance and Nature of Problem Solving

The construction of knowledge best comes about when the learner is confronted with meaningful problems that must be solved. Rather than learning isolated so-called thinking skills, the learner more typically becomes engaged in solving meaningful problems that require the use of generative knowledge and the application of certain problem-solving strategies. This problem solving results in contextualized knowledge—knowledge that is understood in the context of meaningful tasks.

Problem solving as a general approach can be categorized among several types. The following draws from and modifies the typology suggested by Marzano et al. (1997):

- *Decision making:* Decision making answers the question "What should we do?" or "What should have been done?"
- *Investigation:* Investigation attempts to answer the general question "What happened?" It can take several forms: How did this happen and why? What might have happened if . . . ? What will happen?
- *Experimental inquiry:* Experimental inquiry answers the question "How can this phenomenon be explained?" It is the chief method of the empirical sciences.
- *Problem solving:* Problem solving as a specific type involves identifying how a remote goal can be achieved by overcoming

obstacles, such as "How can we reduce the consumption of fossil fuels?"

- *Invention:* Invention is the generation of something that fills an unmet need. It is the use of creativity in fashioning a new product or a new approach.

When solving problems, the learner is experiencing a "cognitive apprenticeship"; by observing and imitating the teacher or more sophisticated peers, the learner is expanding his or her repertoire of problem-solving skills, testing knowledge claims, and developing greater understanding.

Developing Units From a Constructivist Perspective

This issue of unit development is so critical that it requires closer examination. As noted above, there are many models of unit development. The following discussion explicates one process that embodies constructivist principles; the model has worked well in curriculum workshops presented for classroom teachers. (For purposes of greater clarity and directness, the second person *you* is used in this section to represent the unit planning team.) Though the steps below are listed in linear fashion, they should be seen as flexible and recursive. Developers can start at any point in the process and move back and forth.

To guide the process of unit development, you should keep in mind the criteria shown in Table 13.2 and use them to guide your work and evaluate the products. The criteria have been derived from the literature on unit development and modified to accommodate the special nature of constructivism. (The following sources provide useful guidance for the unit development process: Glatthorn, Boschee, & Whitehead, 2006; Henson, 2000; Marzano, 2007; McCombs, 2003; Meek, 2007.)

Block in the Unit. The first step is to block in the unit. The blocking process establishes the general parameters within which the unit will be developed. You make several decisions or confirm some decisions previously made.

- *The title of the unit:* The title should make clear the general emphasis of the unit. The unit being used as an example here will be called "Our Changing Language."

TABLE 13.2

Special Criteria for Constructivist Units

- The unit is outcomes-focused. The unit goal or key outcome is clearly stated; the benchmarks and the lesson objectives are directly related to the unit goal or standard.
- The unit appropriately integrates content from that subject (or from two or more subjects) and makes use of writing and reading as ways of learning.
- The unit emphasizes depth, not superficiality, with sufficient time provided to achieve depth of understanding.
- The unit focuses on problem solving, conceptual change, and critical thinking in the context of real situations.
- The unit has appropriate sequence and coherence so that lessons build on and relate to each other.
- The unit fosters a constructivist approach to learning, one that sees the learner as an active maker of meaning and a cognitive apprentice, using generative knowledge to solve meaningful problems.
- The unit emphasizes a social context for learning and makes effective use of cooperative learning and student interaction.
- The learning activities recommended are directly related to the outcomes, are likely to achieve the outcomes, and are developmentally appropriate.
- The unit makes appropriate provisions for individual differences and is especially sensitive to the needs and strengths of students from minority ethnic groups.
- The unit provides for authentic assessment of learning.

- *The length of the unit:* If you have not previously determined the length of the unit, you should do so at this stage, keeping in mind the importance of curriculum depth. Obviously, you will also consider the students' development stage and attention span. A general rule of thumb is this: the older the student, the longer the unit. In the example chosen, you might tentatively allocate two weeks to this language unit.
- *The unit goal or outcomes:* Each unit should have one to four clearly stated major goals or outcomes. A shorter unit will probably have one goal; longer units may have as many as four. The unit goal is a general statement of what you want the students

to learn by studying the unit. Unlike the benchmarks and the more specific lesson objectives, the unit goal will often be stated somewhat generally. To ensure a problem-solving orientation, you might consider using language that clearly implies a critical thinking orientation. Here are some examples:

o Think critically about television.
o Solve a problem relating to language change.
o Use concepts of semiotics to interpret the culture critically.
o Understand the ecology of the tundra.
o Understand climate change and predict changes.
o Understand how families are changing and predict further changes.

Identify the Problem to Be Solved. In this approach to unit development, you or the students identify a problem or a set of problems to be solved in the unit. It should be noted that some curriculum experts with a constructivist orientation take a different direction here. For example, Blythe (1998) recommends that at this stage, you should identify a "generative topic"—a topic that is central to the discipline, accessible to the students, and connectable to diverse topics within and outside the discipline. That generative topic is then used to derive the goals of the unit. However, the problem focus seems to provide a more direct route to the goal of problem solving.

Problems can be identified in several ways. First, they can often be derived from the unit goals, benchmarks, or more specific grade-level objectives in the curriculum guide. As you review them, you will begin to see interesting problems emerge. You can also think of questions that can lead to problems. Here, the heuristics shown in Table 13.3 may help you.

You can apply those heuristics in two ways. One way is to apply them to a set of themes or concepts, such as the following: family, friends, culture, conflict, regions and places, ethnic groups and genders, eras and ages, environments, and careers. Thus, using Heuristic 5 (What different perspectives do people have about it?) in connection with the theme *careers,* you could identify this problem:

How do the following people view the role of the principal? The principal? The teachers? The students? The parents? The superintendent? The school board?

TABLE 13.3

Curriculum Content Criteria

What is its nature?

1. What is it?
2. What does it mean?
3. What is its structure? How can we make a model of it? What are its parts?
4. How would you classify it?
5. What different perspectives do people have about it?
6. How does it operate?
7. What patterns can be seen in its various manifestations?
8. What is wrong with it, and how would you fix it?

What are its relationships?

9. What are its similarities with and differences from others in its class?
10. What is its quality in comparison with others?
11. What inferences and generalizations can be drawn from it?
12. What are its causes and its effects?
13. How and why is it changing?
14. What were its past forms, what are its present forms, and what will be its future forms?

What are the options with respect to it?

15. What are your values with respect to it?
16. How can it be improved?
17. What are your choices with respect to it?
18. What new forms or uses of it can we create?

You can use those same heuristics in examining the several components of the subject or subjects on which you are focusing. For example, you can apply Heuristic 13 (How and why is it changing?) to the study of communication to identify this problem:

How are electronic media (such as the computer, Internet, cell phones, text messaging, and podcasts) affecting the way we communicate?

You can also engage the students by having them generate questions that they would like to answer. In facilitating this process, you may wish to teach them a simplified version of the same heuristics. After students list several specific questions they would like to answer, you can assist them in grouping the individual questions into problem statements.

Another way to identify a problem is to begin with the materials available. Problem-solving units work best when students can gain access to and use a body of knowledge. If you have a good collection of materials on a topic, such as advertising, you can review it to see what problems it suggests.

After tentatively identifying the problem to be solved, reflect about the unit goal previously identified. Now consider several factors: the time available, the students' knowledge and interests, and the materials available. This reflection process may suggest the need to reframe the unit goal—to modify its general thrust or to make the outcome more sharply focused. In the example analyzed here, the problem of language change seems too broad and demanding for eighth-grade students, particularly considering that only two weeks have been allocated to the unit.

The unit outcome might be reframed in this manner:

Explain how and why the vocabulary of the language changes.

Draft the Unit Scenario. The next step is one not ordinarily found in curriculum texts, but it has been found to be especially effective in working with classroom teachers. The unit scenario is a script for the unit. It explains in general form how the unit begins, how it moves through the stages of learning, and how it ends. It refers to the major ways the students will learn, emphasizing how they will solve the central problem. In brief, before you get into the details of the lesson objectives and activities, you delineate the big picture.

Develop the scenario by first reflecting, imagining, and brainstorming in a somewhat freewheeling manner. As ideas crystallize, jot them down, continuing in this manner until you have a very clear mental picture of the major components and flow of the unit. The final step is to write a clear draft that can guide you and your colleagues. Here is the first draft of the unit scenario for the unit on vocabulary change:

Activate students' prior knowledge by asking them how they think new words come into the language. Then have students interview grandparents or other older people in their lives about words used today that were not used when they were in high school, such as *laser.* Have them use the results to make some preliminary generalizations. Maybe then set up expert groups, each one studying in depth one way that words come into the language. After studying how, move into why—technology, societal changes, immigration patterns. Then have them predict some new words for the year 2020. Close by having expert groups present reports and having students role-play teenagers talking in the year 2020.

When you have finished the first draft of the scenario, you should check it against the criteria for unit excellence. This is only a preliminary check to ensure that you are moving in the right direction.

Developing the unit scenario is a very useful mental process to assist in planning. In many ways, the mental processes are more important than the writing. And the unit scenario helps you do the mental planning. However, the scenario need not be included in the unit itself.

Determine Knowledge Needed and Means of Access. With the scenario in mind, think about the knowledge needed and how students will gain access to that knowledge. Students can best solve problems when they have in-depth knowledge relative to the problem. In this sense, this unit model synthesizes content and process rather than seeing them as separate entities. Students acquire knowledge—then make that knowledge generative in solving the problem. To identify the knowledge needed, reflect on the scenario and then focus on the problem, asking this question: "If I were solving the problem, what knowledge would I need?" Then adapt your knowledge needs to the students' developmental level.

To solve the problem of vocabulary change, students would probably need to have access to two bodies of knowledge: the types of vocabulary change that take place and the factors that affect vocabulary change.

Also, think about the most efficient and effective means for the students to get access to that knowledge. In making this decision, consider the age of the students, the nature of the knowledge, and the materials readily available—or those that you can produce. Here are some ways that students can access knowledge:

- Listen to the teacher present information.
- Learn through guided discovery and discussion.
- Interview experts, parents, and other sources.
- Learn from peers.
- Read texts and other print materials.
- Use computer software and online methods.
- View television.
- Use other media.

These resources for knowledge acquisition provide the raw materials for problem solving; they embody the generative knowledge that students will need to solve the problem. All problem-solving units will require the students to gain access to and use such knowledge resources. Some teachers have found it useful to identify resources early in the unit planning process, because knowledge resources play such a critical role.

In the unit planned here, the following resources might prove useful:

- Collections of new words that have recently come into the language
- Short stories from several periods of our history illustrating vocabulary change
- Articles both bewailing and welcoming vocabulary change
- Teacher-written materials on vocabulary change

Consider How Students Will Solve the Problem. Students should be taught the problem-solving process they will need to solve the problem and then have an opportunity to apply it, both individually and in groups. In the example here, students would need to be taught the principles of inductive reasoning and the skills of predicting.

Determine Which Learning Strategies They Will Need to Learn. Learning strategies are the mental operations that help in the problem-solving process. Some are generic, such as using web diagrams and thinking maps to suggest connections; some are subject-specific, such as listing all the known elements in solving mathematical problems. Subject-specific strategies are better taught in context, not in isolation.

Determine How Students Will Demonstrate Learning. An important piece of the planning process is deciding how students will demonstrate their learning. In fact, experts have pointed out that planning can often begin by deciding how learning can be authentically assessed—then proceed by "teaching to the test." The demonstration may take many forms: publications, dramatizations, visual displays, multimedia presentations, reports, and essays. The essential issue is to ensure that the demonstration of learning is closely related to the goals of the unit.

As noted above, the demonstration in the unit used as an example would take two forms: groups would report on how words come into the language, and students would role-play, using new words they predict will enter the language.

Sketch in the Lesson Plans. With the unit-level planning completed, you now move to the lesson level. But you don't develop lessons from scratch. Rather, you develop them from all the work you have done thus far at the unit-planning level. Thus, a lesson is derived from the unit; a unit is not a random collection of lessons. As you develop lessons, keep the focus on problem solving and conceptual change, using generative knowledge.

Prepare the Unit for Review and Dissemination. The final step is to prepare the unit for peer review and dissemination. Systematize all the previous decisions, add the necessary details, and prepare a review draft of the unit for colleagues to evaluate. Teachers have found the form shown in Table 13.4 useful in systematizing these decisions. The form lists down the left the major components of the unit; across the top, it lists the daily lessons. Thus, a 3-week unit would list 15 daily lessons. (Only a portion of the unit is shown.)

The form has several advantages. It reminds developers and users of the major components of the unit. Viewed from left to right, it shows how a given component develops across the unit. Viewed from top to bottom, it shows the main elements of the daily lesson plan.

SOME CRITICISMS OF CONSTRUCTIVISM

Constructivism has spawned progressivist approaches rooted in Dewey and Piaget's theories. Others, such as Lev Vygotsky, Jerome Bruner, Seymour Paperrt, and David Ausubel, have added new perspectives to constructivist learning theory and practice. For instance, Seymour Paperrt's work has led to the use of computers

TABLE 13.4

Form for Unit Planning and Dissemination

Title of Unit _____   Grade Level _____

Developers _____

Unit Goal _____

Standard _____

Benchmarks _____

Problem _____

Unit component	Lesson 1	Lesson 2	Lesson 3	Lesson 4
Lesson Objectives				
Knowledge Source				
Problem Solving				
Learning Strategy				
Assessment				

and information technology in constructivist environments (Educational Broadcasting Corporation, 2004). Bencze (2007) notes that although constructivism is not supported by everyone, it is one of the most influential educational theories of our time. It is certainly one of several important theories of learning that have affected educators' approaches to teaching.

The constructivist approach places much of the responsibility for learning on students with the teacher as facilitator. It promotes reflective, inquiry-based learning; cognitive based instruction; active, hands-on learning; problem solving, problem-based learning, and project-based learning; and group work. Among the criticisms noted are the following:

- Social constructivism leads to groupthink. The collaborative aspects of constructivist classrooms tend to produce a "tyranny of the majority," in which a few students' voices or interpretations dominate the group's conclusions and dissenting students are forced to conform to the emerging consensus (Educational Broadcasting Corporation, 2004).
- Constructivists, by downplaying evaluation through testing and other external criteria, have made themselves unaccountable for their students' progress (Educational Broadcasting Corporation, 2004).
- Constructivism is elitist.
- Other nonconstructivist but "progressive" educational theories have been most successful with children from privileged environments and backgrounds who are fortunate in having outstanding teachers and committed parents. Disadvantaged children, lacking such resources, benefit from more explicit instruction (Educational Broadcasting Corporation, 2004).

CHAPTER SUMMARY

This chapter continues to focus on how principals can lead the curriculum process in schools through unit development. It provides a rationale for unit development; demonstrates how to organize the planning process; and specifically shows how a constructivist unit might be developed, discussing the specific role of the teacher and the nature of problem solving. Constructivism seems to be more than another fad; it represents a significant break from behaviorist models of teaching and learning. It is a relatively new approach that will probably grow in influence, as schools look for higher student engagement and authentic learning. Constructivism is at the heart of good teaching, and the need to drive up test scores through "drill and kill" techniques should not marginalize its necessity. However, to be effective, it will require curriculum developers to rethink the nature of curriculum units and the processes used to develop them from a constructivist perspective.

REFERENCES

Bencze, J. L. (2007). *Constructivism.* Retrieved October 24, 2007, from http://leo.oise.utoronto.ca/~lbencze/Constructivism.html

Blythe, T. (with the teachers and researchers of the Teaching for Understanding Project). (1998). *The teaching for understanding guide.* San Francisco: Jossey-Bass.

Brooks, J. G., & Brooks, M. G. (1999). *The case for constructivist classrooms* (rev. ed.). Alexandria, VA: Association for Supervision and Curriculum Development.

Cornelius-White, J. (2007). Learner-centered teacher-student relationships are effective: A meta-analysis. *Review of Educational Research, 77*(1), 113–143.

DeVries, R. (2002). *What does research on constructivist education tell us about effective schooling?* (Occasional research paper #5). Cedar Falls: University of Northern Iowa, The Iowa Academy of Education. Retrieved October 24, 2007, from www.uni.edu/freeburg/FreeResources.html

Educational Broadcasting Corporation. (2004). *Constructivism as a paradigm for teaching and learning.* Retrieved October 24, 2007, from www.thirteen.org/edonline/concept2class/constructivism/index.html

Glatthorn, A. A., Boschee, F., & Whitehead, B. M. (2006). *Curriculum leadership: Development and implementation.* Thousand Oaks, CA: Sage.

Gray, A. *Constructivist teaching and learning.* (1997) (SSTA Research Centre Report #97-07). Regina, Canada: Saskatchewan School Boards Association Research. Retrieved October 24, 2007, from http://saskschoolboards.ca/research/instruction/97-07.htm

Henson, K. T. (2000). *Curriculum planning: Integrating multiculturalism, constructivism, and education reform* (2nd ed.). New York: McGraw-Hill.

Marzano, R. J. (2007). *The art and science of teaching: A comprehensive framework for effective instruction.* Alexandria, VA: Association for Supervision and Curriculum Development.

Marzano, R. J., Pickering, D. J., Arredondo, D. E., Paynter, D. E. (1997). *Dimensions of learning teacher's manual* (2nd ed.). Alexandria, VA: Association for Supervision and Curriculum Development.

McCombs, B. L. (2003). A framework for the redesign of K–12 education in the context of current educational reform. *Theory Into Practice, 42*(2), 93–101.

Meek, J. (2007). *Constructivism: A model of learning for preparing problem solvers.* Retrieved October 24, 2007, from the Prentice Hall eTeach Web site: www.phschool.com/eteach/social_studies/2002_12/essay.html

CHAPTER FOURTEEN

Enriching the Curriculum and Remediating Learning

A s district leaders develop the curriculum and as teachers make yearly planning calendars, they should both be aware of the need for the enrichment and remediation that occur at the classroom level. The principal can play a key role in helping teachers develop quality enrichment materials and remediate learning effectively.

HELPING TEACHERS ENRICH THE CURRICULUM

Enrichment is defined here as learning that goes beyond and extends the mastery curriculum. The mastery curriculum is the core curriculum that meets these criteria: it is essential for all students, it is best learned with a great deal of structure, and it is the curriculum likely to be tested. It is the curriculum that the district controls. The mastery curriculum should be designed by the district so that it does not require more than 80 percent of the time available. The remaining time can then be used by teachers for enrichment and remediation. In this way, all students experience an enriched curriculum, rather than its being offered only to the gifted (who need it least of all).

The Nature of the Enrichment Curriculum

The enrichment curriculum lacks the essentiality and importance of the mastery curriculum, but it needs careful planning, primarily to avoid excessive repetition from grade to grade. The enrichment curriculum should be seen as the leaven of the curriculum, providing lightness and excitement and restoring some fun to the curriculum.

Content for the enrichment curriculum can be derived from several sources, as follows:

- Special student interests
- Special teacher knowledge and interests
- Aspects of that discipline not typically studied in school
- New developments in the subject
- Special knowledge of parents and other community members
- Local aspects of a topic that is drawn from the mastery curriculum
- Topics in the mastery curriculum studied in greater depth

Because it is less important, the development of the enrichment curriculum should take a lower priority than the development of mastery units.

General Planning for the Enrichment Curriculum

The first step is to develop school-based policies and general procedures for the enrichment component. Here are the issues to be considered:

- Will the enrichment content be delivered as part of regular courses, or will it be organized as elective courses? If elective courses are used as the means of delivery, how will credits be assigned at the secondary level?
- How much time should be allocated to enrichment? Will enrichment be offered during the regular class period, before school, after school, during a special class period, or in special "enrichment weeks" carved out of the school calendar?
- Who, besides certified teachers, can teach enrichment content: school administrators, district supervisors, aides, parents, other community volunteers, students, university faculty? What policies will govern the use of noncertified personnel?
- What resources will be provided to support enrichment learning?

The next step is to organize multigrade teams for every subject that will use enrichment units. At the higher grade levels, students can provide useful input for such teams. The task of these teams is to develop for that subject a master chart similar to the one shown in Table 14.1. Even in elementary schools using a grade-level organization, the multigrade, single-subject perspective is needed at the outset of the project.

TABLE 14.1

Enrichment Planning for Social Studies

Grades: 6–8

Planners: Harley, Washington, Garcia

Overall Design:

In social studies, the enrichment units will be organized as mini courses requiring six periods of instruction. Students will select one course from the three listed; parent approval will be necessary.

Proposed Units:

Grade 6

- Shopping can be dangerous to your health (integrated unit combining economics and health education)
- Watching the town council in action (civics and political science)
- Centreville in the Civil War (local history)

Grade 7

- Eating across the world (introduction to anthropology)
- Understanding groups in action (elementary sociology)
- Ordinary heroes (multicultural education and history)

Grade 8

- Watching the stock market (economics)
- The economics of clean air (integrated unit combining science and economics)
- You, the beach, and the sea (geography)

A central committee composed of teachers, school administrators, and parents should then review these proposals, checking for the following:

- Do the proposed units enrich the curriculum?
- Are the proposed units developmentally appropriate?
- Do the proposed units avoid repetition?
- Are the proposed units likely to be approved by parents?
- Do the proposed units respond to the special needs of our students?
- Do the proposed units sufficiently provide for integration?

At this juncture, teachers will probably need to devote one session to the development of the enrichment curriculum. Although they can use the unit-planning skills they have acquired, they should be encouraged to see the enrichment curriculum as a special opportunity to be creative. Unlike the mastery curriculum, it need not be objectives-driven, tightly structured, and carefully assessed. The enrichment curriculum is a time for them to try new approaches, test new materials, and bring to bear their special knowledge and interests.

To provide a climate that will stimulate teacher creativity, teachers should be assured that they will not be evaluated while presenting the enrichment curriculum. One simple way of preventing inappropriate evaluation is for the teacher to post a simple "Enrichment" sign when an enrichment lesson is being presented.

Evaluating the Enrichment Curriculum

Though teachers should not be evaluated while presenting the enrichment curriculum, the principal should work with them in assessing the impact of the enrichment curriculum. The assessment should include three major components:

1. A committee should review all proposals and all enrichment units to ensure they are of the necessary quality.

2. Peers should give each other nonevaluative feedback as they observe each other teach enrichment units.

3. Students should be surveyed from time to time to assess their perceptions of quality.

Helping Teachers Remediate Learning

In implementing the curriculum, teachers should work for mastery by all students. To accomplish this goal, they will need to develop their expertise with two kinds of remediation: on-the-spot remediation and systematic remediation.

On-the-Spot Remediation

On-the-spot remediation is the response the teacher makes in every lesson upon becoming aware that students are not mastering the content. The principal should ensure that teachers understand this process.

Frequently Monitor Student Learning

In every class, teachers should monitor learning on an ongoing basis. The monitoring can take many forms: observing students at work, evaluating student products, asking questions, interpreting nonverbal signals of confusion, encouraging student questions, having students write brief statements of what they are learning, and giving brief written quizzes.

Adjust Instruction as Needed

When the monitoring suggests that several students are not mastering the content, the teacher should make the necessary adjustments. These can take many forms, including the following:

- Using a simpler vocabulary to explain key concepts
- Giving more examples of concepts
- Using visual and multimedia representations of the concept
- Taking additional time to explain
- Providing students with concrete experiences using the concept
- Having students who have mastered the concept explain it in their words

In observing instruction, principals should assess the teacher's skill in on-the-spot remediation and provide whatever help is needed.

Systematic Remediation

Systematic remediation is a structured program designed to increase the performance of low-achieving students who need more help than that provided by on-the-spot remediation. By reviewing grades, test scores, and other indices of learning, the principal should work with the teachers in identifying students who need systematic remediation.

Rather than adopting some quick-fix program, the principal should work with teachers in a problem-solving mode. Here they can use those factors identified from the research and shown in Table 14.2. Brief explanations of the factors follow.

Three of the factors involve out-of-school elements. The first is the extent of parental involvement and support. When parents

---

TABLE 14.2

Factors Accounting for Student Learning

Student Factors

    1. Student age

    2. Student ability

    3. Student motivation

School Factors

    4. Curriculum

    5. Instruction

    6. Use of in-school time

    7. School and classroom climate

Out-of-School Factors

    8. Parent involvement

    9. Peer pressure

    10. Use of out-of-school time

SOURCE: Adapted from Fraser, Walberg, Welch, and Hattie (1987); Walberg (2003).

provide a supportive learning environment at home and become actively involved with the school, student achievement is improved. The second is how students spend out-of-school time. If they spend too many hours watching television and working for pay and too little time doing homework, achievement will suffer. The final out-of-school factor is peer pressure. Especially among minority youth, school achievement is perceived as selling out to the majority culture. Peers often ridicule students who work hard to achieve.

Seven factors involve the school. Three of these relate to the student as a learner. The student's age and developmental maturity influence learning; to a great extent, this is outside the school's control. The student's ability in a subject and prior achievement in that subject also influence learning. The final factor is the student's motivation to learn that subject; low motivation means less learning.

Two factors involve the school's climate. The overall school climate influences learning: students need an environment that is safe, orderly, and learning focused. The classroom climate, in general, should emphasize a task orientation and high expectations for all students and convey sufficient emotional warmth to make students feel known and valued.

The three remaining factors are under the direct control of the school. The first is the amount of time that students are actively engaged in learning. The second is the effectiveness of the teaching methods used: too much teacher talk results in less attention and less learning. The final element is the quality of the curriculum and its potential for engaging students in learning.

The principal and teachers can use the results of this problem analysis to design a systematic enrichment program. A typical program that addresses several of these factors would include the following strategies:

- Providing additional time after school
- Using volunteers as afterschool tutors
- Using materials that provide an alternative route to learning
- Working with parents to develop a supportive home environment
- Providing staff development for all teachers on making the curriculum more meaningful and using more effective teaching strategies

CHAPTER SUMMARY

This chapter emphasizes that teachers should understand that simply implementing the standard curriculum is not enough. They need to enrich the curriculum for all students and provide enrichment and remediation as needed. The chapter describes the nature of enrichment, suggests some planning steps, recommends evaluation strategies, and addresses a systematic plan for remediation. The next chapter addresses evaluation of the curriculum.

REFERENCES

Fraser, B. J., Walberg, H. J., Welch, W. W., & Hattie, J. A. (1987). Synthesis of educational productivity research [Special issue]. *International Journal of Educational Research, 11*(2), 145–252.

Walberg, H. J. (2003). *Improving educational productivity* (University of Illinois at Chicago: Publication Series No. 1). Retrieved October 24, 2007, from www.temple.edu/lss/pdf/publications/pubs2003–1.pdf

CHAPTER FIFTEEN

Evaluating the Curriculum

The curriculum should be evaluated at every step of its development. In determining a schedule for development, the task force should conduct a needs assessment. When the scope and sequence chart is in draft form, they should evaluate it rigorously for consistency, focus, and coordination. As the new guide is developed in draft form, they should evaluate it. The most important evaluation, however, will occur at the school and classroom levels as the principal and teachers cooperate in a rigorous evaluation of curriculum quality. For the evaluation to be useful, however, it should employ a comprehensive framework that includes all the teacher-relevant curricula explained in Chapter 10: the assessed or tested curriculum, the supported curriculum, the written curriculum, the taught curriculum, and the learned curriculum.

EVALUATING THE ASSESSED OR TESTED CURRICULUM

The assessed or tested curriculum usually includes four kinds of tests or assessments of student learning: standardized tests, state tests, district tests, and classroom tests. In evaluating the first three types, the teachers should find that the alignment process explained in Chapter 10 is sufficient evaluation. The single consideration here is the extent of congruence between the test and the written curriculum. If the alignment process indicates a major lack of congruence between these tests and the written curriculum, the district has a clear choice: change the test or change the curriculum.

Helping Teachers Develop
and Evaluate Classroom Tests

Teachers will need the assistance of the principal in developing and evaluating classroom tests. If the principal can help teachers develop more valid classroom tests, both can rely on test results with greater confidence. Developing valid and reliable classroom tests is an important and complex skill. Its complexity is exemplified in a 17-step flowchart developed by Nitko and Brookhart (2006), which shows all the steps that should be taken by test makers in developing a valid achievement test.

Though the process they describe is useful in developing major departmental examinations that have major impact on the student's educational future, it is perhaps too complex and time consuming for making classroom unit tests. What follows, then, is a simplified process that will result in better tests.

Assess the Constraints and Resources. This first step examines some practical considerations: What constraints will place limits on the nature of the test? What resources are available to help the teacher develop the test?

Analyze What Was Taught. There are two useful ways of analyzing what was taught. Berliner (1987) recommends that the teacher develop a two-dimensional matrix. Down the left-hand side, the teacher lists the content areas. For example, the content areas for a unit on the Civil War might include these: causes of the war, alignment of states in the war, significant battles in the war, people who played key roles in the war, and results of the war. Across the top, the matrix classifies the desired behaviors of students. Berliner uses three classifications: knowledge/comprehension, application, and analysis/synthesis/application. The teacher uses the matrix to identify foci for test items. Thus, the intersection of the content area "people who played key roles" with the desired behavior "analysis/synthesis/evaluation" would yield this focus for a test item: "Evaluate Lee and Grant in relation to their effectiveness as generals." (See also Hiebert, Morris, Berk, & Jansen, 2007; Popham, 2007.)

An alternative method that we have used with teachers is illustrated in Table 15.1. This method uses categories of objectives that seem more in keeping with the way teachers conceptualize units: terms, facts and information, big ideas, skills and processes,

TABLE 15.1

Unit Analysis Form

List the terms taught.

- Natural resource, renewable resource, pollution, environment, conservation, water treatment plant, sewage treatment plant, phosphate, algae, solar energy

List the facts and information taught.

- The Environmental Protection Agency is a government agency that monitors compliance with laws.
- Taking a shower uses 95 liters of water; taking a bath uses 133 liters.
- The manufacture of plastics requires the use of strong chemicals and high temperatures.
- Between 2000 and 2007, the world population increased by about 506 million people.

List the big ideas taught.

- The water cycle
- Acid rain

List the skills and processes taught.

- Interpret a table of data.
- Identify common causes of air pollution.

List the learning strategies and problem-solving skills taught.

- Analyze the trade-off involved in requiring factories to reduce pollution—cleaner air results in higher prices for the consumer.
- Explain how one person can make a difference in conservation.

essential questions, critical thinking, and problem solving. It serves the same purpose as the content/behavior matrix; it simply uses different categories.

The unit analysis form can be distributed to students to help them prepare for the test; it can also be used by the teacher as a means of guiding the review work.

Determine Which Objectives Will Be Tested. Most teachers do not want to take the classroom time needed to test everything that appears in the analysis of what was taught. Rather, they should select from the complete list those items that they believe should be tested, considering elements such as the importance of that item for future work, the amount of time that was devoted to teaching it, the resources available, and the time required for testing it.

Determine the Relative Weights of Tested Objectives. The fourth step is to determine relative weights for all objectives to be tested. The weights serve three purposes: they help the teacher prepare the test, they help the student allocate time during the test, and they aid the teacher in scoring the test. The easiest way to indicate relative weights is with a percentage figure.

Write the Test Items. The information collected thus far is now used to write test items. The teacher first determines the type of questions to be used for each objective, weighing both issues of validity (which type will most validly assess learning?) and utility (which type will be easiest to score?). Here, there are several choices: essay question, fill-in-the-blank, or supply-the-answer; true-false; matching; multiple choice; and performance or demonstration. Each of these has its own advantages and limitations.

Essay questions best tap the ability to reason but are difficult to score. Fill-in-the-blank and supply-the-answer are best for sampling knowledge but are a bit more time consuming than other short-answer types, for both the student and the teacher.

True-false questions are easy to score, but they permit guessing, and they do not validly assess many objectives that cannot be so dichotomized. Matching and multiple-choice questions are useful short-answer types but again involve a guessing factor. As explained more fully below, performance tests probably yield more valid information about learning but are difficult to construct and score.

Assemble the Test. In assembling the test, the teacher has several choices about how questions should be ordered and grouped. The teacher can group by content; for example, all the questions dealing with the battles of the Civil War could be grouped together. The teacher could group by behavior desired, gathering all the knowledge-comprehension items together. Bloom, Hastings, and

Madaus (1971) recommend that when the items are relatively homogeneous with respect to content and behavior, it might be desirable to group by difficulty, beginning with the easier questions. Here, question items may be constructed to follow the various levels of the New Bloom's Taxonomy or the Marzano's New Taxonomy, depending on which system is used at the local context. As far as is possible, the test content should match the rigor of the district and state tests. Bloom et al. also note that when different kinds of items are used (such as true-false, multiple choice), it is probably wise to group by type. Doing so makes it easier for the teacher to give directions and the student to follow them.

Write Clear Directions. Test developers should use simple language that the students can read and understand. They should write full directions, not relying on the explanations given orally when administering the test. They should also indicate the point value. Local tests should mirror the format, language, vocabulary, and style of the state assessments to provide practice and orient students to the final state assessments they will be taking. Here are examples of unclear and clear directions:

Unclear: Match the names of the generals with the battles they led.

Clear: Below are listed five generals. Each has a blank space next to his name. Find in the list below the battle that he led. In the blank space, write the letter that is next to the battle he led.

Example: Jones: _d_ (10 points)

Now the teachers are ready to review and revise the test. They should give the test to a colleague and ask him or her to identify any potential problems. They should also review the test to be sure that the directions are clear. As a final check, they should take the test themselves to determine the time required and the clarity of directions.

To emphasize the importance of quality classroom tests, the principal should schedule a conference with each teacher to examine collaboratively a test that the teacher has given and graded and one that the teacher plans to give. The criteria shown in Table 15.2 can be used by the teacher in developing classroom tests and by the principal in assessing their quality.

TABLE 15.2

Criteria for Evaluating Classroom Tests

Format, Style, Directions

- Does the test have a professional appearance and use a clear format?
- Is the test written clearly and correctly, free of spelling, punctuation, and grammatical errors?
- Are the directions clear?
- Are point values clearly stated?

Content

- Is the test comprehensive, sampling all areas covered in the unit?
- Do test items include all levels of complexity, from comprehension to synthesis?
- Does the weighting of test items reflect the importance of the content?
- Do the form and wording of items minimize opportunities for guessing?

Helping Teachers Evaluate by Assessing Performance

Because of growing dissatisfaction with paper-and-pencil tests, educators are increasingly exploring the use of performance, exhibition, or demonstration assessment in which the student is asked to perform or demonstrate competence. Such performance or demonstration measures are typically recommended for evaluation at several levels: at the end of the unit; at the end of the term or year; and at the end of some level of schooling, such as middle or high school.

Sizer (1996) believes that a high school diploma should be awarded on the basis of what he terms an "exhibition of mastery," which requires the student to demonstrate real intellectual accomplishments. Such exhibitions, as he describes them, would be public performances at which the student would prove that he or she had mastered certain broad skills and knowledge bases.

Here, for example, is a performance test that could be used in grades K–4 in mathematics. Students are given a large box of raisins and are asked to estimate the number of raisins. To accomplish the task, they are provided with a balance, containers of different sizes, and a calculator. They must use a second method to check their first estimate and record the results. (This test was cited by Mitchell, 2007, as based on the standards of the National Council of Teachers of Mathematics.)

Wiggins (1989) identifies eight intellectual design features of such demonstrations: essential (not just for a grade), enabling (pointing the learner toward more complex use of skills), contextualized and complex (not discrete skills taken out of context), involving student research, assessing habits and repertoires (not recall or "plug-in" skills), representative (emphasizing depth, not breadth), engaging and educational, and involving ambiguous tasks.

Though the art of developing demonstrations or performance measures is relatively recent, some preliminary writings in the field suggest that a process like the following would be used (for a fuller discussion of the process, see Archibald & Newmann, 1988; Stiggins, 1987, 2007; Wiggins, 1998).

Identify a Major Goal. The initial step is for developers to identify a major educational goal they want the student to achieve at the end of a certain level of schooling. The goal should be a general one that encompasses several component skills and knowledge bases; it should also have educational significance. Suppose, for example, that they want all eighth graders to have achieved this goal: become a more discriminating and critical user of television.

Identify the Behaviors Within the Goal. Next, they should break down that goal into its more specific constituent behaviors. This second step will assist in developing the demonstration measures. As the developers complete this step, they should keep in mind both the developmental level of the learners and the limits of what is attainable in schooling.

Here, for example, are the constituent behaviors that might be identified for the general goal of becoming a more discriminating and critical user of television:

- Limit television viewing to no more than 12 hours a week.
- Use selection tools (such as critics' columns and newspaper schedules) to identify important shows to watch.
- Demonstrate an awareness of how commercials attempt to shape behavior by appealing to basic human drives and needs.
- Evaluate television news shows for objectivity and fairness.

Identify What Will Be Required of the Student. Now the developers should identify the demonstrations or performances required for the student to exhibit mastery. Wiggins (1989) suggests seven structural features here: involve a public; do not rely on arbitrary time constraints; offer known tasks; have the student provide cumulative evidence, such as a portfolio; require collaboration; encourage practicing; and make feedback central.

Here are the demonstrations or performances that the teachers might require for the critical viewing goal identified earlier:

1. You are to present to the class two logs of television viewing: one showing your viewing schedule at the beginning of the school year; the second, at the end of the school year. You will explain to the class the major differences between the two logs.

2. You and four of your classmates will be given a copy of the entertainment section of the Sunday newspaper and a copy of *Newsweek* magazine for the same week. You will be expected to identify five shows that you consider important to watch and explain why you have chosen them.

3. You will be shown videotapes of three commercials for a popular brand of athletic shoes. You will explain in a well-written essay how those commercials are attempting to influence your buying behavior.

Devise the Rubrics. The rubrics are an evaluation guide that lists the levels of performance and the features desired at each level. Then the developers can write a scoring plan to be used in evaluating the performance, including the score recording method to be used. Stiggins (1987, 2007) identifies these score recording methods as possibilities: checklist, rating scale, anecdotal record, portfolio, and audio- or videotape.

Though some have questioned the practicality of such complex performance measures, they appear to be a very promising alternative to paper-and-pencil objective tests.

Evaluating the Supported Curriculum

The supported curriculum includes all the learning materials used to support the written curriculum, including texts and software.

Here again, the alignment process can be useful in determining the congruence between the supported and the written curricula. If major gaps are found, three options are available: purchase other materials, change the curriculum, or develop supplementary materials to fill the gap.

If the principal and the teachers have an opportunity to participate in the selection process, they can use the criteria shown in Table 15.3 to make a more systematic assessment of quality.

TABLE 15.3

Criteria for Evaluating the Supported Curriculum

Format, Appearance, Durability

- Are the materials of high quality in their physical makeup: Are they clearly formatted, attractive to the eye, and made of durable materials?

Style

- Are the materials readable by the intended users but not oversimplified?
- Are the materials free of bias based on gender, ethnicity, and age?

Content

- Does the content suitably reflect the nation's cultural diversity?
- Does the copyright date indicate that the content is current?
- Is the content congruent with the curriculum?
- Does the content provide sufficient depth for the topics treated?

Authorship

- Does the authorship include both scholars in the field and experienced classroom teachers?

Evaluation

- Have the materials been rigorously field tested?

EVALUATING THE WRITTEN CURRICULUM

The written curriculum includes the scope and sequence chart and the district curriculum guide. Once the district developers have produced the first draft of the scope and sequence chart for a given subject, principals and teachers should evaluate it critically, as it provides a foundation for the more detailed curriculum guide. They should use the criteria shown in Table 15.4 as a basis for their assessment.

TABLE 15.4

Criteria for Evaluating Scope and Sequence Chart

- Does the chart appropriately reflect the recommendations of experts and professional groups?
- Does the chart correspond with state standards and state tests where applicable?
- Is the chart easy to read and interpret without excessive detail?
- Does the chart focus on mastery outcomes?
- Is the grade placement developmentally appropriate?
- Do the entries reflect systematic development without excessive repetition?
- Do the entries indicate effective coordination from grade to grade and level to level?

The curriculum guide itself can be evaluated by using the criteria shown in Table 5.1 in Chapter 5.

EVALUATING THE TAUGHT CURRICULUM

The taught curriculum is the curriculum that the teacher actually delivers. An evaluation of the taught curriculum should use three approaches. First, as explained in Chapter 12, the principal should cooperate with the teacher in assessing the yearly plan, using the criteria shown in Table 12.3. Second, as explained in Chapter 13, the principal should collaborate with the teacher in reviewing the units developed, using the criteria shown in Table 13.2.

Finally, periodic observations should be made to determine the extent to which the teacher presents lessons that are derived from these yearly and unit plans and to assess the effectiveness of the delivery. These observations will be of three types. The first two types of observations should be limited to an assessment of the mastery curriculum. As noted in Chapter 14, the teacher's delivery of the enrichment curriculum should not be evaluated.

1. As explained in Chapter 11, informal observations should be made periodically as a means of monitoring the curriculum.

2. Any formal evaluation of teaching by the principal should include one item that refers to implementation of the curriculum; observations for evaluation purposes should include an assessment of this component. Such a criterion might be stated this way: "Implements the district curriculum with fidelity and effectiveness."

3. Peers can observe each other and give objective, nonevaluative feedback focusing on delivery of the curriculum. Such peer observations can be a regular part of a more comprehensive peer-coaching program that enables the observed teacher to determine what the observation will include (see Glatthorn, Boschee, & Whitehead, 2006, for fuller details here). Or the peer observations can be organized specifically for the purpose of evaluating the curriculum as one phase of a comprehensive curriculum evaluation.

   The peer observations for curriculum implementation should give the teacher feedback about this issue alone, addressing three specific questions:

   a. Was the lesson part of a unit that was based on the district curriculum?
   b. Did the teacher make clear how the lesson related to the overall unit by providing appropriate reviews, linking the present lesson with lessons previously taught, and showing its connections with what is to come?
   c. Did the teacher help the students connect with the content, showing its relevance to their own lives?

EVALUATING THE LEARNED CURRICULUM

The most important evaluation question examines the learned curriculum: Have students achieved the learning goals of the curriculum? Two types of evaluation are useful here.

Assessing Student Learning in Every Class

Principals should help teachers assess student learning as a part of every class session. One of the most important uses of evaluation is to guide the instructional process. In this sense, evaluation is not perceived as something separate from instruction; instead, it is conceptualized as an integral part of teaching. In almost every lesson, the effective teacher uses an interactive and recursive process: assess–plan–teach–assess–modify plans–teach. It must be noted that as part of the process of aligning curriculum, instruction and assessment, the development of common assessments by teachers at a grade or subject level is becoming more widespread.

The research on effective monitoring of student learning suggests that the practices shown in Table 15.5 can be used in almost every lesson. To facilitate its use, it is written as a handout that can be copied and given to teachers.

Evaluating Unit Achievement

The other approach to evaluating the learned curriculum is to analyze the results of end-of-unit tests. If the test has been developed by following the procedures explained previously, it should provide a valid measure of student learning. However, teachers will need help in analyzing and using test results, as they typically do not take the time to pursue this approach. Because the analysis of unit test results can be time consuming, principals may want to provide special staff development time for teachers to learn and practice the skill, using a unit test they have administered. The following process should work for most teachers:

1. Prepare a large chart. Across the top, list the major areas covered by the test. Here, for example, is how one teacher analyzed the coverage of a test on the Civil War:
   - Causes of the war
   - Alignment of the states
   - Major battles and their outcomes
   - People who played important roles in the war
   - Results and effects of the war

Down the left-hand side of the chart, list the names of all the students in that class.

TABLE 15.5

Research-Based Practices for Effective Monitoring of Student Learning

1. Begin the instructional session with a brief oral or written quiz that checks student knowledge of skills and knowledge taught in prior lessons. If you use a written quiz, have students check their own work or each other's, emphasizing that the quiz has only an instructional purpose for you and them. If you use oral quizzing, keep your questions and responses brief.

2. As you explain a concept or skill, monitor attentiveness by observing student behavior, remembering that such monitoring does not always yield reliable results. Do not be misled by students who have mastered the art of concealing inattentiveness by giving signals of being on-task.

3. After you have explained a concept or demonstrated a skill, check for student understanding. The easiest way is to ask a few specific questions, being sure not to call on only those who volunteer.

   You can ask younger students to use certain previously established signals, such as "thumbs up/thumbs down" or "hold up one finger if the first answer is correct, two if the second," or to use a handheld response device if the classroom is equipped with modern technology. Alternatively, with reluctant or less able students, you can ask for a group response.

   If you assign seatwork or have students work in groups, monitor their work closely as they learn and, as noted above, hold them accountable for the productive use of time.

   From time to time, evaluate student learning by asking them to write a brief response to a question or to explain their understanding of a concept. Such written responses help students clarify their own understandings and give you useful feedback.

4. Close class with a brief evaluation of what has been learned. You can use several methods for this end-of-class evaluation— conducting a brief oral quiz, using a written quiz, or requiring all students to write a summary of the lesson's highlights.

In addition to using the above guidelines for each class, keep in mind the following general practices.

(Continued)

(Continued)

- Remember that the primary purpose of such evaluation is to improve learning. Use errors as opportunities for learning.
- Follow up the instructional evaluation by providing appropriate feedback to the students and additional help when that is indicated.
- Use the evaluation to modify your own instructional approaches. You should remediate if students have not learned. If it is obvious that most of the students have not understood a concept you just explained, you should reteach, modifying the learning processes.
- As often as you can, build in opportunities for student self-evaluation. You can give self-scoring quizzes. You can use special student-response sheets that reveal the correct answer when the appropriate spot is rubbed. And the computer is ideal as an evaluation tool; it provides instant feedback and effective follow-up.

SOURCE: Table 15.5 draws primarily from Berliner, 1987; Bloom et al., 1971; Good & Brophy, 2000; Guskey, 2003; Jacobs, 2004; Lombardi, 2007; Marzano, 2006.

2. Record on the chart how each student performed on each section of the chart, using one of these symbols:

E: excellent performance

S: satisfactory performance

U: unsatisfactory performance

3. Analyze the results, examining both dimensions—performance by student, performance by area.

4. On the basis of the analysis of results, use one of the following options:
    - Provide for individual remediation if only a few students did not achieve mastery. Proceed with the next unit for the entire class.
    - Provide for group remediation if several students did not achieve mastery. Delay introducing the new unit; let achievers work on enrichment content.
    - Reteach the whole class as needed if most of the students did not achieve mastery. Let achievers serve as peer tutors.

Chapter Summary

This chapter focuses on how to evaluate the tested or assessed curriculum and the supported, written, taught and learned curricula. It also addresses how to develop class tests, evaluate assessment performance, and measure student learning in class and unit achievement. The curriculum evaluation process explained here is comprehensive but time consuming. Principals should use it flexibly, depending on their assessment of need and the immediate value of its probable results. In the next, concluding chapter, we summarize how principals can fit together all the separate curriculum activities discussed in this book in an integrated, comprehensive process that becomes part of the habits of mind of successful curriculum leaders.

References

Archibald, D., & Newmann, F. (1988). *Beyond standardized testing: Authentic academic achievement in the secondary school.* Reston, VA: National Association of Secondary School Principals.

Berliner, D. C. (1987). But do they understand? In V. Richardson-Koehler (Ed.), *Educators' handbook: A research perspective* (pp. 259–294). New York: Longman.

Bloom, B. S., Hastings, J. T., & Madaus, G. F. (1971). *Handbook on formative and summative evaluation of student learning.* New York: McGraw-Hill.

Glatthorn, A. A., Boschee, F., & Whitehead, B. M. (2006). *Curriculum leadership: Development and implementation.* Thousand Oaks, CA: Sage.

Good, T. L., & Brophy, J. E. (2000). *Looking in classrooms.* New York: Longman.

Guskey, T. R. (2003). How classroom assessments improve learning. *Educational Leadership, 60*(5), 6–11.

Hiebert, J., Morris, A. K., Berk, D., & Jansen, A. (2007). Preparing teachers to learn from teaching. *Journal of Teacher Education, 58*(1), 47–61. Retrieved October 28, 2007, from http://jte.sagepub.com/cgi/content/abstract/58/1/47

Jacobs, H. H. (2004). *Getting results with curriculum mapping.* Alexandria, VA: Association for Supervision and Curriculum Development.

Lombardi, M. M. (2007). *Authentic learning for the 21st century: An overview.* Retrieved October 30, 2007, from the EDUCAUSE Learning Initiative Web site: www.educause.edu/ir/library/pdf/ELI3009.pdf

Marzano, R. J. (2006). *Classroom assessment and grading that work.* Alexandria, VA: Association for Supervision and Curriculum Development.

Mitchell, R. (2007). *Testing for learning: How new approaches to evaluation can improve American schools* (paperback ed.). New York: Free Press.

Nitko, A. J., & Brookhart, S. M. (2006). *Educational assessment of students* (5th ed.). Upper Saddle River, NJ: Pearson.

Popham, W. J. (2007). *Classroom assessment: What teachers need to know* (5th ed.). Boston: Allyn & Bacon.

Sizer, T. (1996). *Horace's Hope: What works for the American high school.* Boston: Houghton Mifflin.

Stiggins, R. J. (1987). *Design and development of performance assessments.* Washington, DC: National Council on Measurement in Education.

Stiggins, R. J. (2007). *Introduction to student-involved assessment for learning* (5th ed.). Upper Saddle River, NJ: Merrill Prentice-Hall.

Wiggins, G. (1989). Teaching to the (authentic) test. *Educational Leadership, 46*(7), 41–47.

Wiggins, G. (1998). *Educative assessment.* Alexandria, VA: Association for Supervision and Curriculum Development.

PART V

Looking Ahead

Chapter Sixteen

Curriculum Leadership

Putting It All Together

The preceding chapters have taken an analytical approach to curriculum leadership, examining the separate functions that should be accomplished. This chapter summarizes by suggesting how the principal can fit these separate activities into an integrated, systematic, comprehensive design and process.

WORK CLOSELY WITH DISTRICT LEADERSHIP

Though this work has been centrally concerned with curriculum work at the school level, it has also emphasized the critical role of the state and the district. It is especially important for the principal to work closely and collaboratively with district leadership in the ways indicated rather than acting independently. Close cooperation can perhaps best take place within a formal, school-based management program. Though the research indicates that school-based management is not associated with student achievement, it seems to result in a higher level of innovation and to have a positive effect on teacher morale, at least in the initial years (see Glatthorn, 1996; Heck, Brandon, & Wang, 2001).

It should be mentioned that in this book, we assume that the principal's role as curriculum leader is not simply to respond to a curriculum handed down by the state or district; rather, the principal's role is actively to help to shape and influence the final curriculum to be implemented by the school. Once the principal has led the curriculum process and engaged the stakeholders in the school, the principal's role then becomes that of instructional leader. The curriculum leadership role and the instructional leadership role are not mutually exclusive: the curriculum is the foundation on which instruction is built.

SET UP THE CURRICULUM ORGANIZATIONAL STRUCTURES

With a cooperative relationship established with district leadership, the first step is to organize for curriculum improvement. Each school will have its own committee structure, but the one illustrated in Figure 16.1 has worked for many schools. A School Leadership Council serves as the central group, the basic decision-making body in a school-based management approach. It develops an overall school improvement plan, which is revised each year. To carry out the curriculum-related tasks, a Curriculum Task Force is appointed. It works collaboratively with the Instructional Teams, which are organized by grade level in the elementary and middle schools and by department in the high school.

Figure 16.1 Organizational Structures

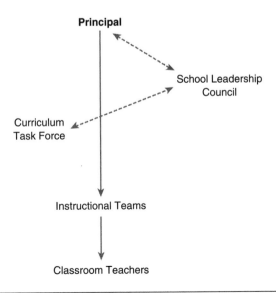

Use Team Leadership

Though this work has emphasized the importance of the principal's role, several reasons suggest the need for the team approach described in Chapter 3. First, a team approach makes the principal's job more manageable by spreading the tasks among others. Second, a team approach is an effective means of harnessing the talents of others rather than relying solely on the abilities of administrators. It subscribes to the culture of teacher leadership. Finally, the team approach is more likely to build support among teachers by involving them in the decision making.

Make Curriculum Improvement Part of an Overall Plan

Curriculum improvement has its greatest impact if it is an integral part of an overall school improvement plan. Schools are complex interacting systems: changing one aspect has a ripple effect on the remaining parts of the organization. An example is the current interest in the 90-minute block schedule. In one high school that was audited, the school implemented a new block schedule without changing the curriculum or providing staff development to help teachers change the way they taught. The result was unfortunate: the teachers used the first 45 minutes to present the standard curriculum and then used the second block of time for student seatwork.

Use an Incremental Process in Effecting Curricular Change

Though there are strong pressures for radical school improvement, the research indicates that incremental change is the most effective approach. Experts in the change process who have reviewed the research conclude that the most effective change occurs when leaders hold big dreams while taking small steps to accomplish them. After reviewing the histories of high schools that had accomplished significant change, Louis and Miles (1990) and Louis, Febey, and

Schroeder (2005) concluded that it is best to start small, experiment, and expand the successful changes while contracting the less successful. The advice seems especially sound when considering curriculum change. Developing and implementing a new curriculum will take two to three years if high quality and effective implementation are to be achieved. The process cannot be hurried. However, the NCLB system and state accountability systems expect schools to show dramatic progress.

PRIORITIZE CURRICULUM TASKS

The order in which curriculum tasks will be carried out is determined by several factors: (a) the requirements of the school improvement plan, (b) the internal relationships of the functions, and (c) the school's special needs, among others. If the importance of the change is the sole criterion, the following priorities would be assigned:

High Priority

1. Develop the school's program of studies.

2. Develop a learning-centered schedule.

3. Monitor and assist in the implementation of curriculum.

Middle Priority

4. Align the curriculum.

5. Help teachers develop a yearly planning calendar.

6. Help teachers develop units of study.

Lower Priority

7. Develop the school's vision and goals.

8. Determine the nature and extent of curriculum integration.

9. Help teachers enrich the curriculum and remediate learning.

10. Help teachers evaluate the curriculum.

USE ROUTINE ACTIVITIES TO SUPPORT QUALITY CURRICULA

The evidence indicates that effective principals carry out the same tasks as less effective principals (Lee, 1987; Lee & Smith, 2001). The difference is that effective principals use these routine activities as a means of fostering school improvement, while less effective principals carry out those same activities in a rote manner. Here are some examples of the ways in which principals can use routine activities to support the curriculum:

- While monitoring the student cafeteria, ask students about their perceptions of what they are studying.
- In making informal observations, focus on curriculum implementation.
- Organize informal lunch seminars with teachers to discuss current curricular issues.
- When report cards have been issued, talk informally with teachers about the impact of curriculum on student achievement.
- In evaluating teacher performance, include an analysis of the teacher's implementation of the curriculum.
- Use a part of each faculty meeting as an opportunity to support the new curriculum.

DEVELOP SPECIFIC PLANS AND MANAGE TIME

Effective principals do their best to plan systematically and manage their time to accomplish their goals. They control their time, setting priorities and blocking out the time needed to accomplish their goals. Less effective principals, on the other hand, move from crisis to crisis without clear goals, letting others determine their schedules. They sit in the office, waiting for the next conference or crisis, as a steady stream of parents, teachers, and students consumes the time available. Though the unpredictability of school life makes it impossible to develop rigid plans and control all the hours of the principal's day, it is possible—and necessary—to set clear goals and build a flexible schedule that includes quality time for curriculum leadership.

To illustrate a process that can be used, assume that the School Leadership Council has assigned to the Curriculum Task Force the responsibility of planning and directing a project to renew the school's program of studies (see Chapter 7 for the details). Principal Marcia Howard works with the council in developing an action plan similar to the one shown in Table 16.1.

TABLE 16.1

Action Plan: Renewing Program of Studies

General Goal: To fine-tune the present program of studies so that it leads to a better educated student body.

Actions	Responsible	Start	Finish
Secure initial approval of superintendent	Howard	8/1	9/1
Develop the knowledge base	Henrico	9/1	12/1
Disseminate, discuss knowledge base with faculty	Howard	1/5	1/12
Identify constraints, resources	Smiley	10/1	11/15
Design comprehensive evaluation	Howard	1/15	2/1
Carry out evaluation	Haskins	2/15	5/15
Review evaluation results and report to faculty	Henrico	6/1	6/15
Plan special workshop to develop proposed changes	Howard	6/30	7/1
Hold special workshop	Howard	8/15	
Prepare report for parent, superintendent, board review	Howard	10/1	10/30

Howard then reviews the plan and lists the tasks for which she is chiefly responsible:

- Secure initial approval of superintendent.
- Disseminate, discuss knowledge base with faculty.
- Design comprehensive evaluation.
- Plan special workshop to develop proposed changes.
- Hold special workshop.
- Prepare report for parent, superintendent, and board review.

She notes the starting and finishing date for each responsibility. She then takes each major responsibility and breaks it down further into its component steps. Thus, for the first step, she makes this mental list of what has to be done, knowing the superintendent's decision-making style:

1. Write memo to superintendent requesting conference and summarizing tentative plans.

2. Schedule conference with superintendent.

3. Hold conference.

4. Write follow-up memo.

For each of those specific steps, she assigns a target date and enters that in her planner.

The planning styles of individual principals will vary, of course. The important concerns are to set specific goals, break them down into actions to take, and build a schedule to accomplish them.

A Personal and Concluding Note

We view this book chiefly as a practical handbook for principals, assistant principals, and aspiring principals that spells out the leadership skills needed to establish a quality school-based curriculum. Yet the book should not be concluded without emphasizing the leadership dispositions and attitudes needed to inspire and cooperate with classroom teachers—the prime deliverers of the curriculum. This includes working within the parameters established by the union and teacher contracts. The attitudes discussed below may be much more important than any set of skills.

A Determination to Act Ethically. Since NCLB was introduced, several articles have appeared in the national press reporting massive cheating by principals who fraudulently changed and falsely reported test results. Predictably, excuses were offered by the principals and their supporters: too much emphasis on test scores, fear that their schools would look bad, concern for disadvantaged minority students. However, there is no excuse for unethical behavior. In all things, act ethically.

A Focus on Results. All that really matters is the learned curriculum. Even the taught curriculum should be seen as a facilitating element, not the primary goal. However, from our perspective, legitimate results go beyond test scores. The following student outcomes, among others, also matter: increased motivation to learn; a positive attitude toward the school, the teachers, and other students; the ability to resolve conflicts productively; and a disposition to act ethically.

A Belief in Teachers. Although too many teachers have low motivation and an excess of self-concern, our many years of teaching have persuaded us that an overwhelming majority of teachers are conscientious professionals who want the best for the children and youth they teach. Curriculum development should be based on a foundation of trust: trust that teachers want to conform with federal, state and district regulations; trust that teachers want to be successful; trust that teachers want to help all students achieve success; trust that teachers want to produce quality curricula.

A Concern for Accountability That Goes Beyond Test Scores and AYP. All those involved with the schools should be held accountable for their actions: the community, in providing support; parents, in being productively involved; the school board, in developing learning-centered policies; district leaders, in fostering school-based decision making, developing and implementing a learning-centered budget, and training school administrators; school administrators, in providing learning-centered leadership; teachers, in improving the quality of the curriculum and instruction; and the students, in making the best use of quality teaching. To limit accountability to principals and teachers is manifestly unfair and unwise. Principals and teachers should be held accountable for those elements they can control. But one of the elements that has the greatest impact on student achievement is educational financing, a factor over which principals and teachers have very little influence.

High Expectations for All. Leadership, curricula, instruction, and assessment should all be based on realistically high expectations for students—a sincere belief that all students want to learn and can learn. Those high expectations also apply to self, to teachers, and to parents. These are trying times for educators, when "teacher bashing" seems to be a popular indoor sport. Despite these antagonistic forces, all of us need to be realistic optimists who hope for the best and learn from the worst.

CHAPTER SUMMARY

This chapter emphasizes the systems approach to curriculum improvement in which the school leader must work closely with the district leadership. A special plan must be developed and organizational structures must be in place to support a systematic process for curriculum, including the use of team leadership within the school (as opposed to random acts of curriculum improvement). Curriculum change is seen as an incremental process in which the school prioritizes the curriculum tasks and manages time appropriately and the principal uses routine acts to support curriculum quality. The chapter concludes by identifying essential leadership attitudes, such as strong ethical behavior, focus on results, concern for accountability, belief in teachers, and high expectations.

The role of curriculum leader, shaping what is taught and tested, is not optional for principals; it is an essential, high-value role, especially in the NCLB era and beyond. Strong, intentional leadership in curriculum development is a necessity for strong instructional leadership.

REFERENCES

Glatthorn, A. A. (1996). *School based management: A policy analysis.* Greenville, NC: School of Education, East Carolina University.

Heck, R. H., Brandon, P. R., & Wang, J. (2001). Implementing site-managed educational changes: Examining levels of implementation and effect. *Educational Policy, 15*(2), 302–322.

Lee, G. V. (1987). Instructional leadership in a junior high school: Managing realities and creating opportunities. In W. Greenfield (Ed.), *Instructional leadership: Concepts, issues, and controversies* (pp. 77–99). Newton, MA: Allyn & Bacon.

Lee, V. E., & Smith, J. B. (2001). *Restructuring high schools for equity and excellence: What works.* New York: Teachers College.

Louis, K. S., Febey, K., & Schroeder, R. (2005). State-mandated accountability in high schools: Teachers' interpretations of a new era. *Educational Evaluation and Policy Analysis, 27*(2), 177–204.

Louis, K. S., & Miles, M. B. (1990). *Improving the urban high school: What works and why.* New York: Teachers College.

Index

**CORWIN
PRESS**

The Corwin Press logo—a raven striding across an open book—represents the union of courage and learning. Corwin Press is committed to improving education for all learners by publishing books and other professional development resources for those serving the field of PreK–12 education. By providing practical, hands-on materials, Corwin Press continues to carry out the promise of its motto: **"Helping Educators Do Their Work Better."**